TEN
Vietnamese

TEN
Vietnamese

>>>>> by <<<<<

SUSAN SHEEHAN

 Alfred · A · Knopf

NEW YORK · 1967

£ 3.30

THIS IS A BORZOI BOOK
PUBLISHED BY ALFRED A. KNOPF, INC.

Published February 20, 1967
Second Printing, March 1967
Third Printing, March 1967

Library of Congress Catalog Card Number: 67–11129

Manufactured in the United States of America

Chapter i appeared originally, in slightly different form, as an article in *McCall's*.

Chapter iii appeared originally in *The Sign*.

Chapters vi and x appeared originally as articles in *The New Yorker*.

for C. M. S.

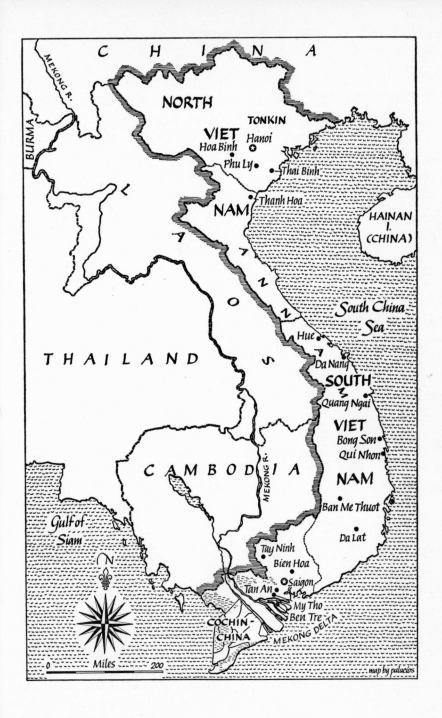

CONTENTS

INTRODUCTION

Saigon, August, 1966

In July, 1965, my husband, a foreign correspond-
ent for *The New York Times,* was assigned to the Saigon bureau of the *Times.* A month later we had set up
housekeeping of a sort in the Hotel Continental, in the
heart of the city.

Most of the three hundred journalists in Saigon work
for newspapers, wire services, weekly news magazines, and
television networks. With the ever-increasing American in-
volvement in the war, Viet Nam has become more of an
American than a Vietnamese story. A reporter's contacts
with Vietnamese are usually limited to the country's leaders
and would-be leaders—a few generals, Buddhist monks, government spokesmen, and free-lance politicians—and to Saigon's waiters and taxi drivers. In the course of doing a piece
on South Viet Nam's refugees or civilian war casualties, a
reporter might interview a dozen of the homeless or injured,
but the individual lives of the subjects would be outside
his story.

From the point of view of daily or weekly journalism
it is understandable that few of the ordinary people of Viet

Nam are written about: they don't hold press conferences, they don't command troops, and they don't plot coups d'état. They are unable to speak English or French, and they lack the services of interpreters. To me their absence from most accounts of the war seemed regrettable. It was these Vietnamese—the people I've heard called "the ninety-five per cent that don't count"—who interested me, for the war is being fought over them and they are its chief participants and chief victims.

Since I was fortunate enough not to have to cover daily stories, I could spend my time roaming the countryside, seeking out the people I wanted to interview, but I still had to cope with the not-so-ideal local working conditions.

Language was a formidable obstacle. Vietnamese is a multitonal, monosyllabic tongue in which an innocent-looking word like *ba*, depending on how it is chanted, can have a dozen meanings. It would have taken me my whole year in Viet Nam to begin to speak even pidgin Vietnamese, so in my reporting I enlisted the aid of a young Vietnamese, Nguyen Ngoc Rao. Rao, who interpreted for me in nine of the ten interviews in this book (I used a Rhade-English interpreter for the montagnard), proved an excellent choice. He has a good command of colloquial English and Vietnamese and a talent for striking up a conversation with strangers and persuading them to reveal themselves.

Transportation was another difficulty. Roads in South Viet Nam are always unsafe, with the exception—during daylight hours—of a few short stretches of the country's main highways. I traveled by road in military convoys until I realized that the trucks and soldiers were more a temptation for a Communist to set off a mine or spring an ambush than a guarantee of safety. A civilian car seemed to attract much less unwanted attention. One such car I hired, however, broke down in the middle of nowhere. Every black-pajama-clad farmer in the rice fields along the highway suddenly looked very ominous. The driver got the car going before any part-time guerrillas (who, when not fighting, till the fields like ordinary farmers) approached us, but from then on I hitched rides in helicopters to cover short distances. For long trips military planes were the only feasible conveyances. Accredited journalists were allowed to travel on them free of charge, and the pilots were capable and courageous; but here the advantages of flying with the military in Viet Nam ended. I flew around the country in a variety of planes; none of them were jets and very few were pressurized. My fellow passengers were sometimes seventy-odd Vietnamese soldiers, properly begrimed and odoriferous after a week in the field, and sometimes crates of pigs and chickens bound for the cooking pots of some remote outpost. The flying weather in Viet Nam is frequently bad and the airstrips are often closed in. When the planes in which I was traveling were forced to fly low because of this, the Viet Cong used them for target practice.

If planes in Viet Nam bear little resemblance to Boeing 707's, Viet Nam's hotels bear even less resemblance to Hiltons. There are two or three adequate hotels for civilians in Saigon, but the few hotels in outlying cities that once were passable have long since been taken over by the U. S. Army and turned into billets; the sleazy establishments that remain are now used for purposes other than sleeping. On my travels I usually stayed at the local American military compound.

xiii

Other problems that I encountered in Viet Nam could not be dealt with as readily as language, transportation, and accommodations. I was eager to talk with as wide a variety of people as possible—soldiers, peasants, and city dwellers, and people of different religions, financial circumstances, and political persuasions. Unfortunately it was impossible to make contact with certain people. My applications for a visa were ignored by North Viet Nam, so I was unable to talk to anyone still living in the North. It would have been foolhardy to venture into a Viet Cong hamlet in the South Vietnamese countryside in the hope of talking to some peasants who had lived under Communist rule for a number of years; while their stories might have been fascinating, I might not have returned to tell them.

Some subjects were easier to come upon than others. Rao and I wandered into hamlets, refugee camps, and Army bases and started talking to people at random until we found a person we wanted to interview at length. The hardest subject to arrange to see was a North Vietnamese prisoner. I first sought an interview with a prisoner through official American channels. I learned over an exasperating period of three months that the same American officers who were so quick to tell journalists that the morale of the North Vietnamese troops was very low, were not willing to produce a prisoner who might prove their case. I finally sought the help of a Vietnamese friend who is a high-ranking government official. With the graciousness the Vietnamese often display to foreigners, he found a prisoner for me the following day. After I had interviewed the young man during a period of several weeks, I understood why the American colonels had declined to produce a North Vietnamese captive.

I carried out the interviews between October, 1965, and May, 1966, writing them as I went along, and I finished the book in July, 1966. I have taken the liberty of letting the word "now" cover a period of seven months—nothing, after all, happens simultaneously. I have changed the names of my ten Vietnamese out of respect for their privacy and in some cases their safety. Where I have used the names of their relatives or friends, hamlet and village names, or such identifying details as the name of the monk's pagoda, I have changed these, too. All city and province names are real. I have used as few statistics as possible, and these with great reluctance and only where they seemed essential for context, since statistics in Viet Nam are notoriously unreliable. I have given the rate of exchange of the Vietnamese piaster as one hundred to the U. S. dollar for the sake of simplicity and because this rate was a realistic one during my first months in Viet Nam. I am afraid that there is no accurate way to convey the worth of the piaster in terms of the dollar. The piaster is undergoing a serious inflation, and its purchasing power varies considerably from one part of the country to the next.

In an introduction a writer is always tempted to try to give the reader the details he could not include in the text. I am tempted to describe how my subjects, far from being frightened by what for most of them was their first conversation with a foreigner—and a foreigner who asked all sorts of impertinent questions at that—were surprisingly hospitable, outspoken, and nonchalant. One subject even dozed off for her afternoon nap in the middle of a conversation. But I must suppress the temptation, because I cannot speak about my subjects nearly as well as they can speak for themselves.

I

>>>>> *N_{guyen} Thi Lan* is a South Vietnamese peasant. She doesn't know her exact date of birth but it says on her identity card, which she cannot read, that she was born in 1910. She was born in An Binh hamlet, a cluster of about a hundred huts set amidst the rice fields, canals, and swamps of the Mekong delta, the flat, green, rich area south of Saigon, and she still lives in An Binh. War has been going on around her for much of the last twenty years—there is now a bullet hole in the wall of Lan's thatched hut—but she has never thought of leaving An Binh and in her fifty-six years she has rarely traveled farther than three miles from her hamlet.

Lan's parents were born in An Binh. They worked in the rice fields and they were very poor. They were never able to buy or rent any land and always worked for land-lords as day laborers. Lan had many brothers and sisters. Her memory isn't good and she can't remember exactly how many but most of them died of illness a long time ago. Only Lan, one younger brother, and one younger sister survived.

Lan's father died when she was a small child. After her father's death, her mother supported the family by working in the rice fields and collecting fish, crabs, and vegetables in the canals. Her mother could not afford to let her go to school. When Lan was eight, she had to start earning her own living by tending a neighbor's two water buffalos; the neighbors fed her and supplied her with two sets of clothes a year. She had a rough time keeping her two charges from eating young rice, which they preferred to the grass they were supposed to consume. "I got thrown from the buffalos' backs many times," Lan says. "I think I can still feel the results of those falls." She tended buffalos for six or eight years, before going to work in the rice fields, and now looks back on this period as the best time of her life. "Buffalos are easier to take care of than children," she says.

When she was about eighteen, Lan was engaged to a young man about twenty-one years old named Tran Van Hieu, who lived a couple of hundred yards away from her in An Binh. Hieu's father came to Lan's home one day and asked her mother to give her up. Her mother agreed. After their engagement was announced, Hieu worked for Lan's mother for a year, cutting wood and doing other chores, to prove he was a hard-working man, worthy of her daughter. The engaged couple had seen each other in the fields since they were children, but they were very bashful and never spoke before their marriage. "We didn't dally in the rice paddies the way young people do today," Lan says. When they were married, Lan and Hieu built a hut of their own in An Binh and they have lived in it, remodeling it occasionally, for the last thirty-five years. Lan's

4

younger brother and sister are also married and live in An Binh. Her mother lives with her son.

Twelve children were born to Lan and Hieu in their hut. Five died when they were very young. Lan can't recall the individual deaths but her children all died of natural causes, not in the war or in accidents. Her seven living children, two sons and five daughters, range in age from sixteen to thirty-four. All of them except her sixteen-year-old daughter are now married and have children of their own. "I had a real hard time with my kids when they were small," Lan says. "My relatives helped me with them so that I could work in the rice fields all day, but I had to rush home to feed them lunch and dinner, and at night I had to husk rice, wash the children and their clothes, and clean my home before I could go to sleep. The children were a burden but heaven gave them to me and I accepted them. I didn't beat my children very much. I used soft words to educate them. I was very overworked and thin when I was young." Lan is still a slender woman, about five feet tall. She wears her black hair pulled straight back from her forehead and tied in a small bun in the back. Her customary attire is a pair of billowing black satin trousers and a well-patched white cotton overblouse; she usually goes barefoot but wears a glazed conical hat when she goes outside. Her face and arms are wrinkled from years of work and exposure to the sun.

Lan and Hieu now share their hut with their youngest daughter, one of their two married sons, his wife, and their four small children. One pig, five chickens, and two pigeons have the run of the hut and are constantly underfoot, foraging for food on the packed earth floor. The pig was bought

5

at the market three months ago and will be sold at a slight
profit in five more months if he survives the epidemics that
have killed most of the other pigs the family has tried to
raise; his diet includes rice bran, which is expensive, but
while he is around he serves as a good garbage disposal. The
chickens will be eaten if they live; five of the ten baby
chickens the family purchased a month ago have already
died of disease. The pigeons are purely ornamental. The
family's three water buffalos, a male, a female, and their
baby (the first of three offspring to survive, thus far)
are confined to a shed outside the hut. The buffalos are
descendants of a pair Lan and Hieu bought some years
ago. They earn their keep plowing the rice fields.

Lan and Hieu's wooden-frame hut measures fifteen by
thirty feet and consists of two large rooms. It has no electricity. There is a cooking area beside the hut, where food
is heated over bricks and wood, and a latrine stands about
fifty feet from the back of the hut over a branch of a canal.
One large room is furnished with several wooden plank
Vietnamese beds. The second large room also contains two
beds but it is used in the daytime as a living room and is
cluttered with tables and chairs, hammocks, mirrors, calendars, family photos, pictures, and three altars. Lan and
Hieu are members of the Cao Dai religion, a mixture of
Buddhism, Confucianism, and Taoism, with lesser amounts
of Catholicism, Indian mysticism, and animism; and whose
saints include Victor Hugo, Joan of Arc, and Dr. Sun Yat-
sen. The main altar is the Cao Dai altar; the other two are
for the worship of Hieu's ancestors—one for his parents,
one for his grandparents. Lan and Hieu's sons and grand-
sons will be expected to worship them after their deaths

and to build altars in their honor. Lan and Hieu have already posed, in rented formal clothes, for the unsmiling photos that will be placed on top of these altars. Lan eats no fish or meat six days a month, as her religion prescribes, and she goes to temple twice a month if she is not too busy working in the rice fields. There is no Cao Dai temple in An Binh (population 719), one of the six hamlets that make up An Khanh village (population 3,898), but there are temples in two of the other hamlets in An Khanh. Lan travels to the other hamlets in her village on foot or by sampan, only to go to temple or to visit a sick relative. She hardly ever goes to any of the other villages in Thu Thua, one of the six districts that make up her province, Long An. She occasionally goes to market in Tan An (population 25,000), the provincial capital of Long An, two and a half miles away from An Binh. Highway 4, the main road from Saigon to the delta, goes through An Khanh village. The entrance to An Binh is just off the highway and Lan's hut is three hundred yards from the road. An Khanh is thirty-five miles southwest of Saigon, an hour's ride on Highway 4. Lan has gone to Saigon only ten times in her life, never for pleasure, but only when someone in the family was very ill and in the hospital there. (The last time she went to Saigon was about a year ago when one of her sons-in-law was seriously injured by a mine.) She is dazzled by the capital and admires its lofty buildings, its cars, and its crowds.

Lan is better off than her mother was. She and her husband have never been able to buy land, but for the last few years they have been able to rent an acre or two and they now spend part of their time cultivating their rented land and part of their time working as day laborers.

7

Lan and Hieu work almost every day during the rainy season, June to November in the delta, when the rice fields must be sown, plowed, fertilized, irrigated, and weeded. They go harvesting for a few weeks in December and then are idle until the next rainy season begins. When they work as day laborers they work a twelve-hour day, from sunrise to sunset, for which Lan is paid forty piasters (about forty cents) and Hieu fifty piasters. They carry their own provisions for breakfast and lunch to the fields because they each receive ten piasters less if they eat the meals provided by their employer, and that is extremely uneconomical for them. Their buffalos work during the rainy season, pulling a plow. The buffalos work only half a day, never a whole day, and are paid thirty-five piasters each for a morning's work. "The buffalos are better paid than I am and that's to be expected," Lan says. "There are fewer buffalos than workers in the hamlet and the buffalos do the heavy work that I can't do." In the rainy season, Lan and Hieu eat three meals a day; in the dry season, when they spend most of their time sitting around the hut, they eat only two.

When the crops are average, the land Lan and Hieu rent provides enough rice for the family to eat for the whole year, after they have paid their landlord his share of the crop. When the crops are excellent, they have some rice left over to sell. When the crops are poor, as they have been for the last two years because the rains have come late, they have to ask their landlord to lower the rent. The landlord has always agreed to lower the rent a little, but they have still had to buy several hundred pounds of rice in bad years. Having to buy rice upsets their budget. The family's cash income covers only their youngest daughter's school ex-

penses, the occasional chancey purchase of a pig and rice
bran to feed it, and the purchase of salt, *nuoc mam* (a spiced
fish-oil sauce used to flavor rice and other food), clothes,
and materials for repairing the hut. They have had no new
clothes for the last two years because of the poor crops.
Lan and Hieu are usually in debt by the end of the dry
season, even if the crops are average. They don't plan on illness, and at least one member of the family falls ill every
month and requires a visit from a practitioner of oriental
medicine. Lan and Hieu now owe ten thousand piasters to
neighbors, relatives, and money-lenders.

Lan could afford to send her first six children to school
only for a couple of years each so that they could learn
how to read and write. Her youngest daughter has finished
all five years of primary school in An Khanh. She is now in
her third year (of seven) in secondary school and is the first
person in the family ever to learn a foreign language—
French. There is no secondary school in An Khanh village
so she goes to school in Tan An. "My youngest child can
get a little better education than the others because I don't
have to feed as many children as I used to," Lan says. Her
daughter attends a government school, which is free, but
she has to provide her own notebooks and textbooks. Lan
also gives her five piasters a day, often a great strain on the
budget, four for transportation from An Binh to Tan An
and back, one for an iced drink. "I'll let my daughter study
as long as she wants to, or as long as I can afford to send
her to school, or until I marry her off," Lan says. "My husband and I arranged for the marriages of our two sons and
we gave up our first four daughters when other families
asked for them. They all married people from An Binh or

9

the other hamlets in our village, and they all live in An Binh. I've never declined a request and I'll give up my youngest daughter when anyone asks for her. We must arrange marriages for our children. I'd like to give them some freedom in deciding who they want to marry, but I insist on having the last say. I want to be sure that my children don't wind up living with unprincipled people."

In recent years, An Binh has been less peaceful than some of the approximately fourteen thousand hamlets in South Viet Nam, more peaceful than others. It was quiet until 1945, when the Viet Minh, the Communist-led guerrillas, began fighting the French Army, which was attempting to reestablish French colonial authority in Indo-China when the Japanese occupation ended. The fighting in the Mekong delta, which formed the greater part of France's colony of Cochin-China, was much less intense than in the central and northern parts of the country, the French protectorates of Annam and Tonkin. In the delta, the Viet Minh ambushed French convoys, terrorized Vietnamese loyal to the French, staged repeated hit-and-run attacks against hundreds of small outposts established by the French along the canals and roads and among the hamlets, and controlled much of the countryside, especially at night. The French held only their outposts (which they were afraid to leave after dark), the larger villages, and the district and provincial capitals. There was no fighting in An Binh itself during the First Indo-China War, perhaps because of its proximity to the provincial capital of Tan An, but the hamlet was not safe enough at night for the prosperous landlords, many of whom supported the French, to stay there; they retreated to Tan An each evening. Poor peasants like Lan and Hieu, who did not support the French, were not bothered by the Viet Minh and stayed in the hamlet. "We didn't take sides," Lan says. "We didn't understand what the fighting was all about. We were only interested in our field work."

After losing the battle of Dien Bien Phu in May of 1954, France signed the Geneva Agreements with the Viet Minh in July. The Agreements, which ended the First Indo-China War, partitioned Viet Nam at the seventeenth parallel. The northern part of the country became the Democratic Republic of Viet Nam (DRVN), now commonly referred to as Communist North Viet Nam, under President Ho Chi Minh, the leader of the Viet Minh. (President Ho had originally proclaimed the DRVN in 1945, at the outset of the war against the French, as the government of all Viet Nam.) The southern half of the country became the Republic of Viet Nam in 1955 after Ngo Dinh Diem, at that time its prime minister defeated Bao Dai, the former emperor of Viet Nam, in a referendum and became the first president of the republic, which is now known as South Viet Nam.

In the early years of his rule, Diem showed promise. He crushed the private armies of the minor religious sects and the bandit lords who controlled organized crime in Saigon, restored administration to most of the countryside, and began reconstructing the war-wrecked economy. During the late nineteen-fifties, however, the régime grew increasingly authoritarian and unpopular, discredited by maladministration and corruption. In May of 1963, President Diem, a Roman Catholic, fell into dispute with the Buddhist hierarchy. The Roman Catholics, who number about 1.7 million of South Viet Nam's sixteen million inhabitants, had been favored by the French colonial authorities because they were anti-Communist and politically reliable. Diem continued this policy to prop up his own government. The number of Catholics in important government positions was far out of proportion to the size of their community. The Buddhists, the religious majority in South Viet Nam, regarded Catholicism as a foreign religion imported by western colonialism and were resentful of the privileges accorded the Catholics. The Buddhist leaders were able to arouse hitherto latent discontent with the Diem régime. The anti-government campaign they launched created the conditions for a successful coup d'état by the South Vietnamese Army. President Diem was overthrown and assassinated on November 2, 1963. Since Mr. Diem's demise there have been eight governments in Saigon, including the current military junta led by Lieutenant General Nguyen Van Thieu, the chief of state, and Air Vice Marshal Nguyen Cao Ky, the prime minister. Under the terms of the Geneva Agreements, about eighty thousand Viet Minh troops in the South were transported to the North over a three hundred day period while French forces in the North progressively withdrew to the South. (The French troops left South Viet Nam in 1956.) The Geneva Agreements also stipulated that there would be free movement of population between both parts of the country during this grace period—about eight hundred and sixty thousand refugees, the majority of them Roman Catholics, fled South to escape the Communists—and that an election would eventually be held to reunify the temporarily partitioned country.

Lan has never heard of the Geneva Agreements. She does not know that her country has been partitioned. The words "North Viet Nam" and "South Viet Nam" mean nothing to her; she only knows that she lives in Viet Nam. She has heard the names Ho Chi Minh and Ngo Dinh Diem but she says she does not know who they are or where they are now living. She has not heard the names of any of the generals or politicians who have headed the eight governments in Saigon since Mr. Diem's death. (Lan's youngest daughter doesn't know anything about the leaders of North Viet Nam or South Viet Nam either; the family has no radio, she cannot afford to buy newspapers, and politics is a forbidden subject at school.) Lan remembers that the French left—she doesn't know quite when—and that she was glad, because the hamlet became quiet again; even the landlords decided it was safe enough to return.

The countryside did not stay quiet long. In 1956, President Diem refused to hold the countrywide elections provided for by the Geneva Agreements, which were supposed to lead to the reunification of Viet Nam. Mr. Diem was uncertain of his own position in the South (he even banned the traditional hamlet and village elections, a very unpopular move) and he believed that the Communists would rig the elections in the North. The Communist leaders in Hanoi, the capital of North Viet Nam, who had hoped to reunify the country under their own rule through such elections, then decided to attempt to take over the South by force. When the Viet Minh fighting troops were withdrawn in 1954, thousands of Communist cadres were left behind, instructed to hide their weapons, and to maintain a clandestine political organization. In 1957, this clandestine organ-

13

ization was ordered to begin political agitation and guerrilla warfare against the Diem government, and the Second Indo-China War was under way. In the early stages, the Communist effort was confined largely to propaganda. The Communist cadres promised the peasants they would drive out the landlords and distribute their land, and eliminate the corrupt government officials. Then the assassinations began. The terrorism was always selective: the Communists murdered either the very competent or the very corrupt village and hamlet officials, the former because they were few and a threat to the Communists and the latter because their execution made the Communists popular with a segment of the peasantry. For every village and hamlet chief or police officer killed, ten others were frightened into silence or cooperation. This combination of blandishment and terror was very effective; it succeeded in destroying the government structure at its most important level in a rural Asian country—in the hamlets and villages where three quarters of the population lives. The central government gradually lost contact with the population. Viet Minh cadres who had been transported North in 1954 were given additional training and infiltrated back into the South to strengthen the clandestine political organization, direct its activities, and help recruit new followers. By 1958, armed bands of guerrillas had been formed. The Mekong delta and other parts of South Viet Nam reverted to the state of affairs during the First Indo-China War. The guerrillas resumed attacks on outposts, this time manned by government troops rather than French soldiers, ambushing convoys, mining roads, and raiding pro-government hamlets. The landlords in Lan's village once again went to Tan An to sleep. Communist control spread slowly and deliberately. The guerrilla bands grew into companies of eighty to a hundred men and then into battalions of three hundred men. By 1961, the year the police chief in Lan's village was killed by the guerrillas, the Communists were threatening to take over the country.

In this new war, the former Viet Minh at first referred to themselves simply as the underground revolutionary movement. By late 1960, the Communist leaders in Hanoi were certain enough of the movement's progress both to remove some of its clandestine nature and to seek to give it a mantle of legitimacy; on December 20, 1960, the formation of the South Viet Nam Liberation Front, the political arm of the guerrillas, was announced. The Saigon government, in an attempt to discredit the guerrillas in the peasants' eyes, soon dubbed them with the title "Viet Cong"— Vietnamese Communists—which was quickly abbreviated to "VC." Lan has heard the term "Viet Cong," but she does not know what Communism is and she refers to the guerrillas either as "Viets," an abbreviation of Viet Minh, or as "liberation people." She refers to the government soldiers and officials as "nationalist people." She understands the new war vaguely as a struggle for the leadership of the country between the liberation people and the nationalist people. She knows that the Americans are helping the nationalist people, but she doesn't know why. She has not heard of anyone helping the liberation people; the words "North Viet Nam," "China," and "Russia" mean nothing to her.

Throughout 1962 and 1963, the fighting in the Mekong delta became more intense and the Viet Cong progressively succeeded in destroying the government administration and substituting their own shadow government in the hamlets, villages, districts, and provinces; their hierarchy was parallel to the government's. The Diem government received a vast amount of American economic and military aid, including thousands of American advisers, helicopter units, and fighter-bombers to support its Army, but, because the Diem government was incompetent, unpopular, and corrupt, all of this proved of no avail. A massive government effort to reestablish control of the countryside, called the strategic hamlet program, which was an attempt to fortify each hamlet, organize the population within it against the guerrillas, and carry out social and economic reforms to win the support of the people, was a failure. The strategic hamlet program was overambitious and badly administered, although it was directed by Ngo Dinh Nhu, one of Diem's brothers and the most powerful member of his government, which was actually a family oligarchy often referred to as the Ngo family regime. By the time Diem fell, in November of 1963, the Viet Cong controlled, in one fashion or another, seventy to eighty per cent of the Mekong delta and over ninety per cent of Lan's province of Long An. An Binh, which had been a strategic hamlet, was more or less under Viet Cong control, although Communist dominance there was not solidified because of An Binh's proximity to Tan An and to Highway 4, which was patrolled by the government Army.

Two of Lan's four sons-in-law and one of her two sons are in their twenties. In 1962, when An Binh was made a strategic hamlet, the young men were persuaded to join the Self-Defense Corps, a government militia formed of men recruited from and stationed in their own hamlets, villages, and districts. Lan's other son and her two other sons-in-law are in their thirties and work in the rice fields; so far they have been considered a little too old for military service. Some of Lan's neighbors have all their sons in the VC; some have sons on both sides—one son was talked into joining or was drafted by the VC when they controlled the hamlet in 1961, another son went into the government Army because he reached draft age when An Binh was a strategic hamlet a year later. Lan has no ill feelings toward her neighbors whose sons are in the Viet Cong. "Taking sides is largely a matter of chance and taste," she says. "I wouldn't join either side myself." It was a VC mine that injured Lan's son-in-law (and killed several of his comrades) when they were traveling in an Army truck on Highway 4 south of An Binh a few months ago, but she bears no animosity to the VC because of the incident. "I can't afford to resent the Viets because my son's injury is beyond my control," Lan says. "It's useless to be angry. It's a waste of emotion. I have to bear the consequences of the war. I don't understand the war but I can't do anything about it. I might as well save my words and feelings."

The majority of the fighting in the Second Indo-China War took place in the delta in 1962 and 1963. In mid-1964, the brunt of the war in South Viet Nam shifted to the central coastal plains and the central highlands north of Saigon. The Viet Cong had accomplished their major aims in the delta—they controlled most of the delta outside the district and provincial capitals and had at their disposal abundant food supplies, manpower resources, sanctuaries to hide in when government troops came after them; and an extremely effective intelligence network—and they

were now intent on concentrating their major efforts elsewhere, as part of their overall strategy of progressively weakening the central government to bring about its final col-
lapse. The war in the delta settled down to sporadic fighting;
since the end of 1964, the government has made only hesitant efforts to regain control of the thousands of lost
hamlets.

The population of Lan's province, Long An, one of the
forty-three provinces in South Viet Nam, is about four hundred thousand. There are now approximately ten thousand
government troops stationed in Long An. About twenty-
eight hundred of these are local militia, formerly called the
Self-Defense Corps and now called "popular forces." Thirty-
two hundred are "regional forces," who are recruited and
stationed in their own provinces. Four thousand are soldiers
of the Army of the Republic of Viet Nam (ARVN), the
national Army, the best-trained, best-equipped, best-led, and
best-paid of the three forces. Government intelligence officers believe there are thirty-two hundred Viet Cong in
Long An. Some of them are in the VC main forces (comparable to ARVN), some are VC regional forces (comparable to government regional forces), and some are VC
hamlet and village guerrillas (comparable to government
popular forces). The only American ground combat troops
in the delta are stationed in two provinces west of Saigon, although American units move to other delta provinces from
time to time for operations against the Viet Cong; almost
all the U. S. ground combat troops, which began to arrive
in South Viet Nam by the tens of thousands in the summer
of 1965, are stationed in the provinces north of Saigon
where they have been fighting the VC and, recently, some

regiments of the People's Army of (North) Viet Nam (PAVN), which have infiltrated into South Viet Nam. The only American servicemen on permanent duty throughout most of the delta are the advisers to the Vietnamese forces and government officials, and the personnel of several helicopter companies who lend support to the Vietnamese troops. In Long An province there are sixty-five American advisers, about half of them stationed in Tan An. An American soldier visits An Binh perhaps once in several months. "When I see an American soldier I feel very sorry for my people," Lan says. "We are so small, and dark, and underfed compared to Americans. Life must be very good and the work must be very easy where they come from. I wonder why they want to come to this poor place."

In mid-1964, the government controlled very few hamlets in Long An. In recent months, the government has attempted to "pacify" some of the hamlets in the province, one by one. This is a lengthy and fragile process which begins when regular Army or regional force troops clear the hamlet of any main-force Viet Cong units operating out of it. Lightly armed pacification teams composed of administrative, psychological-warfare, and health workers, protected by militiamen, are then sent in to uncover and destroy the clandestine Communist control cells in the hamlet, familiarize themselves with the population, and make an effort to win the people's support, recreate a hamlet administration, supervise the construction of hamlet fortifications, and recruit twenty to fifty militiamen from the local population to defend the hamlet. The process can be severely disrupted at any point by a successful Viet Cong attack.

More than eighty per cent of the area of Long An province (and an equal share of the rest of South Viet Nam's countryside) is still controlled or otherwise dominated by the Viet Cong. The government claims it controls about fifty per cent of South Viet Nam's population; in Long An it claims only sixteen per cent. Of the approximately six hundred hamlets in Long An province, seventy-six have been pacified thus far. Others range from those completely under VC control to those hamlets the government hopes to pacify soon. Many VC hamlets are being bombed by American planes and shelled with artillery along with VC bases, but are otherwise being ignored by the government.

The only way to really pacify a hamlet would be to station several hundred troops in it, an impossibility. In Long An, as in the rest of the country, the government does not have enough troops to establish the ten to one ratio that most military strategists consider necessary to put down an insurgency. In Long An, the ratio is only three to one. It is easy for the VC to select a hamlet or an outpost defended by only twenty to fifty government troops, to mass several hundred attackers, and to surprise and overwhelm it in the night. It is also easy for them to snipe at military vehicles on the road and to mine the roads. Highway 4 is often mined, yet it is considered one of the safest roads in South Viet Nam in the daytime (not a single highway in the country is safe at night)—at least from Saigon to the city of My Tho, thirteen miles south of Tan An. At night, the Viet Cong sometimes set up roadblocks on Highway 4 and stop vehicles to search them and their passengers. At night, the American advisers based in Tan An, do not go out of the city. It was mortared by the VC in late December, 1965.

An Binh has been one of the pacified hamlets in Long An since December, 1964. One other hamlet in An Khanh village is pacified, four are not. Two years ago, an American would not have gone to An Binh in broad daylight without an escort of troops. To an American, An Binh's status as a pacified hamlet means that the hamlet is usually safe to enter in the daytime, unarmed, if he stays close to the part of the hamlet near Highway 4 and does not make his visit known ahead of time. VC informers (the government has not found a way to uncover them) know of his presence within a few minutes of his arrival, but are unlikely to do anything about it because there is too great a risk of retaliation by government forces in the daytime. At night, an American might well be killed if he stayed in An Binh, and the VC might murder the family he stayed with, to assert themselves. To government officials, a pacified hamlet is one in which they can live, even after dark, if they are careful to take such precautions as sleeping in a stockade or in a different house every night. Lan has never heard the expressions "strategic" or "pacified" hamlet. She has never been in danger of being murdered by the Viet Cong. To her, the fence that went up in 1962 and then again in 1964 meant that there was less fighting in the hamlet, at least for a while, and thus less chance of getting caught in the crossfire. She likes fences because they connote less fighting to her, but the shooting never stops entirely. The VC subject pacified hamlets to attacks, acts of terrorism, and harassment to undermine government control and to demonstrate to the population that the government cannot protect them. The Viet Cong have attacked An Binh once and terrorized it once in recent months.

One night in August, 1965, the hamlet chief of An Binh was murdered by the VC, who came to his house, took him outside, and shot him in a nearby field. Like many government hamlet chiefs, the one in An Binh rarely slept in his own house, but he did on that particular August night and somehow the VC knew it. The militia were elsewhere in the hamlet at the time of his murder. The hamlet chief's death occurred near the other end of the hamlet and Lan didn't hear the shots. She learned of his death the next morning when his daughter walked past her hut weeping. American advisers in Tan An make a connection between the hamlet chief's murder and a government-constructed irrigation canal officially scheduled to open the morning after the murder; the hamlet chief was supposed to help inaugurate it. Lan says she does not know why he was killed, and neither does the hamlet chief's widow. "I was sorry about the death because he lived in the same hamlet I did," Lan says. "But he wasn't one of my relatives." A new hamlet chief has since taken his place.

One night in October, 1965, a company of VC troops entered An Binh and started shooting. No one is altogether sure of their intentions, but the American advisers in Tan An think that the shooting was a diversionary tactic and that the Viet Cong's main purpose that night was to attack the other pacified hamlet in An Khanh, across Highway 4. The Viet Cong entered An Binh; one militiaman and two civilians were killed before the VC fled. Lan heard the liberation people shouting outside her house and she heard the shooting, but she didn't see anything because she crawled under her bed and covered herself with a blanket until the shooting was over. (She had done the same thing the previous year when there was a skirmish in the hamlet; that time she found a bullet hole in the wall of her hut when she eventually crawled out.) Hieu went to the scene of the October shooting the morning after it occurred; he was so horrified by seeing the pools of blood that he returned home immediately. "My husband went to the funeral of the three people because they were neighbors," Lan says. "I felt sad."

Lan knows the name of the new hamlet chief (she also knows the name of the biggest landowner in the hamlet), but she doesn't know the names of her village chief, her district chief, or her province chief. She doesn't like to be asked questions about people she doesn't know or about a war she understands rather hazily. "If you want to ask something about my country, ask people who have traveled," Lan says. "People who go around to do business have many opportunities to widen their knowledge. I have always stayed at home with my children and my grandchildren and done my routine work, so how can I know anything? Living here is like living in a jug. I've never been to the movies or to the theater. I just hang around my home. I'm very ignorant."

Lan doesn't know who will win the war, or when the war will end, but she is very tired of it and hopes it will end soon. "I would like the war to end because I hate hearing shooting and artillery and planes and bombs," she says. "I don't like to find bullet holes in my walls. I'm very much afraid of getting killed when there is shooting. I'm planning to dig a hole to take refuge in. I'm always anxious and tense. I can't sleep well at night. When there's shooting, you never know if you'll get hit or killed. I've heard that a bomb was dropped on a hamlet somewhere near here the other day.

23

A couple of people were killed and all their furniture was damaged. But my field work is not affected by the war. If the crops are good, I can make ends meet. If not, I have to beg the landlord to lower the rent and borrow some money so that my family will have enough to eat."

>>>>> *Vu Van Phan* was born in June, 1925, in Tuong Nam, a village fifty miles southeast of Hanoi, in what was then the French protectorate of Tonkin and is now the Democratic Republic of Viet Nam. His parents were prosperous landowners. Phan's father supervised the peasants who cultivated his extensive rice fields; he never had to work in the fields himself.

Phan was the only boy in the family. His parents, who were Catholics, had sixteen or seventeen children, but all except Phan and five girls died of illness when they were infants. At the age of twelve, Phan started primary school in Tuong Nam. After three years he was sent to the provincial capital; it took him four years to get through the last two years of his primary education because much of the teaching was done in French and his village French was very weak. In 1945, he had to drop out of secondary school at the end of his first year because of the political, social, and economic chaos resulting from the Japanese occupation and the Viet Minh uprising. He went home and spent a year

27

helping his father supervise the field work and simply idling.

In 1946, Phan's parents arranged his marriage. His family and a very rich Buddhist family in Tuong Nam had been feuding for several generations and seemed on the verge of physical blows. Phan's father thought a marriage might soften the traditional hatred between the families and asked the Buddhist family to let one of their daughters marry Phan; the family consented. Phan's bride was baptized shortly before their wedding took place in the village church in January, 1947.

Shortly after his marriage, Phan became a teacher. He taught the first two grades of the village primary school until early 1948, when the Viet Minh, who by then controlled the area, tried to force him into one of their organizations. Phan was a dreamer and didn't like the prospect of regimentation. He refused to join the Viet Minh organization and his refusal cost him his teaching job. Once again he drifted, this time for a year and a half.

Toward the end of 1949, French troops established an outpost a mile and a half from Tuong Nam, a predominantly Catholic village. In 1945, the villagers had been told by their priests that the Viet Minh were atheistic Communists and very few of them had sided with the Viet Minh. The villagers feared a Viet Minh attack and asked the French for weapons. With the small arms the French gave them they set up a forty-man militia, of which Phan was a member. They were able to defend themselves against small Viet Minh attacks for several months, but one night the Viet Minh sent four hundred well-armed men to crush them. The French were afraid to leave their outpost at night and it was all the village militia could do to hold out until dawn when the Viet Minh withdrew and the French soldiers came to Tuong Nam. The villagers asked the French to give them machine guns so that they would be able to withstand large Viet Minh forces. The French were too suspicious of all Vietnamese to give them the weapons, but the French agreed to take the militia and a few other prominent men from the village into their outpost. The women, children, and older men stayed in Tuong Nam. Immediately after Phan's departure for the outpost with the militia, the Viet Minh came to Tuong Nam and plundered many houses, including his. The Viet Minh then took charge of the village and let the women and children stay there, without physically harming them.

Phan lived in the outpost for half a year and in 1951 left for Hanoi, which the French controlled. Many of his friends remained in the outpost and joined the French Army, but Phan didn't care for military life and hoped to avoid it by going to Hanoi, where he took a job as a secretary in a construction company. His family lived in Tuong Nam until mid-1953, when Phan's father was taken to a Viet Minh jungle prison camp for indoctrination and died of illness—a result of bad living conditions there. After the death of Phan's father, Phan's wife, their first two children, his mother, and his widowed mother-in-law came to Hanoi.

In August, 1953, Phan enlisted in the Army. There was a draft system at that time and he was afraid of being drafted and sent to the front, so he signed up for the signal corps, figuring it would be safe. He had good connections and was accepted. After two weeks military training and two months training in signal operations, he was stationed in his own province in late 1953, but before his division had seen much action, defeat appeared imminent and his division began to withdraw to the relative safety of the big cities. After the country was partitioned, many of Phan's comrades gave up their Army careers and returned to their villages, but Phan realized it would be impractical for him to try to live under the Communists—they were trying to undermine his religion and they had already confiscated all his land—so he decided to stay in the Army. In October, 1954, he left North Viet Nam on a French military ship with his family and his unit. Phan's old division was dissolved soon after he reached South Viet Nam and he was assigned to a new division being formed, but he was able to stay in the signal corps. He was stationed in several parts of South Viet Nam between 1954 and 1957, when he was assigned to Saigon. He has worked in Saigon at various military switchboards ever since.

"Military life was more or less forced upon me and I chose the signal corps because it was the safest in the Army," Phan says. "I've asked twice in recent years to get out of the Army because I don't care for my work. My requests have been turned down. It's almost impossible for a soldier on regular status to get out of the Army, but I'm still hoping to get discharged one of these days. I'd like a secretarial job in the civil service and the government is pretty good about securing such jobs for veterans. I now have to work on a shift basis and that means I sometimes work days, and sometimes nights, and I often have to work on Saturdays, Sundays, and holidays. Civil servants work five and a half days a week and have all Saturday afternoons, Sundays, and holidays off. As a civil servant, I'd get only five thousand five hundred piasters a month—two thousand a month less than I'm getting now—but I'd rather have more interesting work and more freedom. I'm lucky enough to be able to take a pay cut because I own two houses and I have an outside income of eleven thousand piasters a month. I get one thousand piasters a month by renting half of one of my houses to a nasty Vietnamese couple, and ten thousand piasters by renting most of my second house to five nice American GIs and their five Vietnamese concubines."

When Phan was assigned to Saigon, in September, 1957, he and his family were given quarters in his unit's garrison. In early 1958, while walking from his quarters to his switchboard, Phan passed a swamp filled with water lilies in the northeastern section of the city. He spotted a sign saying that the swampland was for sale. People were just starting to build homes in that section and the land looked like a good investment to Phan. With some money he had saved, he bought four hundred and thirty square yards of land, had it reclaimed, and built two six-room houses on two hundred and fifteen square yards (he eventually sold the other two hundred and fifteen square yards of land at a profit). Each house was a concrete, one-story structure divided in half with three small, dark rooms in each half. In late 1958, Phan put up "For Rent" signs outside the two houses. He soon had two Vietnamese families living in the front house paying a thousand piasters a month each, and two Vietnamese families in the smaller back house paying five hundred piasters a month each. Occasionally, a tenant moved

31

away or was evicted for not paying his rent. The tenants were easily replaced—the war had brought many people to Saigon and in recent years has created a serious housing shortage in the capital.

From 1958 to 1961, Phan, his wife, his mother, his mother-in-law, and his growing family (by 1961 he had six children) lived in the garrison. His quarters measured twelve feet by thirty feet; he couldn't get any more space. In 1961, when the two families occupying his front house moved away, Phan and his family moved into the other half. They were slightly less cramped in these three rooms than they had been in the garrison.

Gradually, the former swamp became a bourgeois neighborhood. Most of its residents are minor government officials and Army officers. In 1964, they succeeded in using their influence to get the city to provide electricity and running water (they are still trying to get paving for the dirt road that meanders through the neighborhood) and Phan decided to tear down his two houses and to put up one big, elegant house. The tenants in the front house refused to budge, reneging on the agreement they had made in 1961 to move out whenever Phan gave them a few months notice. The tenants in the back house obligingly moved away soon after they were asked to leave, so Phan tore down the back house and replaced it with a nicer one in August, 1964. The new house, a two-story model, has six bright bedrooms with balconies. Phan decided to rent four of the rooms out for two thousand piasters a month each and to keep two rooms for his family, as well as the three rooms in the old front house. A sign quickly drew tenants. For the first few months, he had Vietnamese living in the new house, but one day in the fall of 1965, when there were two vacant rooms, an American soldier with a Vietnamese girl on his arm came by and applied for one of the rooms. Phan rented it to them. A few days later, a friend of the first GI came with a Vietnamese girl and took the second vacant room. Soon afterwards, the Vietnamese in the other two bedrooms moved away and two more GIs and their Vietnamese girls moved in. Phan thought he had a full house, but one day when he came home from work he found that his wife had been talked into taking in a fifth GI and his Vietnamese girl although that meant the family had to give up one of their bedrooms in the new house. Phan's family now includes seven children; he hopes that number is final.

Phan, a tall, lean, soft-spoken man with a long face, long teeth, and an absent-minded gaze, spends most of his time off from work at home. He reads the newspapers, keeping up with the latest political and military developments, and he likes to sit around. Occasionally, he and his wife go to the theater, or to a movie, or out to dinner with friends from the signal corps or with relatives in Saigon. Phan doesn't socialize with his neighbors; he is a sergeant and the Army officers and government officials in the neighborhood outrank him. The neighbors haven't made friendly overtures to him and he is hesitant to start friendships with them, for fear of being thought a social climber. Phan and his family are not on speaking terms with their unmovable Vietnamese tenants, but they are on excellent terms with the "concubines," as Phan calls them, and he and his family enjoy gossiping with and about them. The concubines have made his life interesting and he would much rather talk about them than about his dull job at the switchboard.

"The concubines aren't bad girls," Phan says. "They're country girls. They came to Saigon when the countryside became insecure. When they first arrived, they took jobs as servants in Vietnamese households, but they were overworked and underpaid. When the American soldiers began to come over here in droves, hundreds of bars opened up and the girls went to work in them. The life of a bar girl wasn't all they'd hoped it would be. The girls aren't especially pretty, they don't speak English, and the competition for soldiers was fierce. They didn't do very well, but they were lucky. After a few weeks in the bars, each of the girls met a GI who took a fancy to her and came in regularly to buy her tea-whiskeys and to bring her occasional presents, and after several months of knowing each other, the GIs asked the girls if they wanted to live with them and the girls said 'Yes.' They all came here to live a few months ago. The girls still don't speak English—the soldiers interpret that as a sign of innocence—and the soldiers don't speak a word of Vietnamese, but they claim they can make themselves understood in sign language. One of the girls is more enterprising than the others. She bought a Vietnamese-English dictionary and keeps it on the bed. With the help of the dictionary, she learned that her GI is a cook. The others don't know what sort of jobs their soldiers have. They do know that they make about two hundred dollars a month. Four of them are privates and one is a sergeant. The concubines haven't been able to find out whether their soldiers

34

have wives back home. I think some of them must because they're not too young. The soldiers told the girls their names, but the girls have forgotten them. The soldiers either call the concubines by their names or call them 'you.' The GIs give the girls about seven thousand piasters a month besides the room rent. All of the girls help support their families. Some have families in the countryside and some have families in Saigon. One concubine's father is dead, and she originally came to Saigon with her mother and her younger sister. They live here with us too. They sleep on the balcony of the concubine's room. The GIs sometimes bring the girls expensive presents like radios. The girls discourage gifts, except cosmetics, because they'd rather have more money. The girls buy gold with the money they don't need. Gold doesn't depreciate and piasters do. The girls hope that with the gold they save they'll be able to buy a little shop when the soldiers leave Viet Nam in a few months. They doubt they can save enough money and they are afraid they'll have to go back to work in bars. The girls dread the GIs' going home. They love their men even though there have been no wedding ceremonies. The girls say the GIs are much nicer to them than Vietnamese men. The GIs sometimes get drunk, but even then they don't shout at the girls; they just go to sleep. It's a good arrangement for the girls—this life is easier for them than sitting up late in bars and it's better for the GIs too. They work irregular hours, but whenever they come home they find their girls waiting for them. The GIs are very jealous of the girls; when the girls go out without them, they go out in pairs. They have little to do—they keep the rooms clean and

35

do the GIs' washing and ironing. The GIs are stationed in Saigon and eat at their billets; the girls eat their meals in restaurants or sometimes with us. They're always welcome to eat with us. They're like elder sisters to my children."

A young man has just built a large house across the street from Phan. He has put up a sign saying "No Rooms for Rent" in front of the house, which is exclusively for his family. The young man knows about the situation in Phan's household and is openly critical of him and it. He accuses Phan of closing his eyes to immoral goings-on, of making his family live in cramped quarters for the sake of money, and of endangering his family by taking in Americans, who are the favorite target of Viet Cong bombs and grenades. Phan points out that the new neighbor, who is in his late twenties, has a job with an American firm and earns a handsome salary in dollars, which he converts to piasters at the black market rate of exchange—twice the legal rate. He also says that the only reason his young neighbor has such a fine job (and thus a fine new house) is that he was able to buy official papers enabling him to dodge the draft. "To keep abreast of the rising cost of living caused by the war and by the Americans, you have to deal with Americans if you want to maintain a decent standard of living," Phan says. "I'm not making a fortune or exploiting anyone. I'm just holding my own."

Phan and his family could get by on his salary, but with the extra rent money they can afford better clothes, medical care, and schooling. Six of Phan's seven children are of school age and attend private Vietnamese schools; in addition, the four oldest ones take English lessons because Phan

36

believes a knowledge of the English language will give them more opportunities in life. The children practice their English by talking to the GIs. Phan doesn't think that the situation under his roof is sinful, or that grenades and bombs are likely, and he says the Americans are much better tenants than the Vietnamese—they are tidier, they pay the rent promptly, they bring him cigarettes from the PX, and there is no chance that they might be VC, who could get him into trouble. Many of the Army officers and government officials in the neighborhood are also supplementing their salaries as Phan has done. They have put up new wings on their houses to rent to GIs. Not all of their American tenants drink as quietly as Phan's five and at night their merrymaking can be heard throughout the neighborhood, mingling with the wails of Vietnamese women being beaten by their hen-pecked Vietnamese husbands.

Phan would like to ask his GIs about their country, but he is too lazy to learn English. He has heard about the United States from friends of friends who have been there. What impresses him most about the United States is that there is not too much difference between the lives of the poor and the lives of the rich. He has been told that many workers have their own cars, that it is very difficult to get servants, and that even some generals have to do errands for their wives and carry their shopping bags. He is amazed that Americans don't have to pay enormous bribes to get a telephone, and that American soldiers don't have to do such tasks for their commanding officers as painting their houses.

Phan admits that he leads a good enough life in Saigon, but he finds the city too dirty, too noisy, too crowded, and too impersonal. He prefers the air in the countryside, and the more leisurely and congenial life. He is resigned to living in Saigon for the duration of the war because the countryside is too dangerous. Once there is peace, he plans to sell his houses in Saigon and leave the city, preferably to return to his own village in North Viet Nam, where he dreams of getting back his forefathers' land.

Phan believes the Americans will stay in South Viet Nam, "because President Johnson has promised they will and a man of his stature would not lie." If the Americans stay, he thinks they will not lose the war to the Communists although it may take them several more years to win it. When the war is over, he thinks the Viet Cong and the North Vietnamese should be forgiven and should not be punished because "we are all Vietnamese."

Since he believes the war will drag on, Phan is making plans for the immediate future in Saigon. "I'm still trying to evict the Vietnamese couple in the front house," he says. "Friends have offered to help me get them to move by beating them up—that's the usual Vietnamese way of dealing with tenants who are reluctant to move—but I don't want to resort to violence. I'm soon going to take legal action against them. If I'm lucky, I'll get the couple to move out in a few months, just about the time the GIs' tours of duty in Viet Nam are completed. I'll then move my family into a rented house for a while, pull down the two houses, and build one spacious three-story house on my land. When it's finished, my family will live on the first floor and I'll rent the second and third floors. If I had the house now, I could be getting forty or fifty thousand piasters a month in rent and rents are going up every week. When my house is ready, I'll put up a sign outside and rent the two floors to anyone who can afford to move in. Most Vietnamese will be unable to afford the rents, so I'm almost certain to have American tenants again. Perhaps by the time the house is ready, the concubines will have found new GIs in bars and will move back in."

III

>>>>> *D*uong *Tam* is a refugee. He fled his native hamlet, Gia Hoi, in the spring of 1965, and now lives ninety-four miles from Gia Hoi in a refugee camp on the outskirts of Qui Nhon, a city on the central coast of South Viet Nam, two hundred and seventy miles northeast of Saigon.

Tam was born in Gia Hoi, one of the eleven hamlets in Loc Chau, a village in Binh Dinh province, in March, 1917, when it was part of the French protectorate of Annam. His parents worked in the rice fields for landlords; they were never able to buy or rent land. They were too poor to send Tam, his younger brother, or his two younger sisters to school. Tam is a little sorry now that he cannot read or write, but he wasn't sorry then; he recalls his childhood as the happiest time of his life precisely because he didn't have to go to school. He went to work in the rice fields when he was ten. In his teens he got bored with planting and plowing and decided to try another trade. He went to live with an uncle who ran an ox-cart transportation service in Ban Me Thuot, a city in the central highlands. He earned more money than he had at home and at first enjoyed his new way of life. Then memories of the rice fields began to haunt him and he realized he could never voluntarily stay away from them. After about six years, he returned home.

Tam's family was Catholic. When he was twenty-two, his parents arranged a marriage for him with a sixteen-year-old girl from Gia Hoi; he stole a few glances at his fiancée after they became engaged, but he didn't speak to her until after their church wedding. Of the many children Tam and his wife have had over the years, eight have survived, six boys and two girls. The oldest child is a married daughter of twenty-two, the youngest is a one-year-old boy. Tam hopes he will have no more children. "Eight is enough," he says. At forty-nine, Tam is a diminutive man with curly hair, who wears short-length pants and an overblouse of coarse grayish-brown cotton. The sun and hard work have weathered his face and hands and made them wrinkled and dark. His eyes have a pronounced squint, but Tam says he has had the squint since birth and that he sees very well. His vision has never been tested.

Tam and his wife both worked in the rice fields after their marriage. They worked very hard and they prospered. In time, they bought four acres of riceland and built a large brick house. Their life was peaceful until 1945. French troops had occasionally marched past their village before then, but had never harmed it. Tam had seen some Japanese troops in the early forties; he had had no contact with them. The Viet Minh, however, made their presence known and felt. Tam had some bad experiences with the Viet Minh from the day he first became aware of them in 1945. "They were always asking me to do some work for them for three days and they always kept me working a month," he says. "I wouldn't want the French to return to Viet Nam, but life under the French was better than under the Viet Minh. The French let us alone. The Viet Minh interfered too much in our lives, making us destroy bridges and making us listen to propaganda. They never kept their promises. My younger brother swallowed the Viet Minh propaganda and joined them. He was killed in a clash with French troops in the late forties. I succeeded in evading the Viet Minh draft. Things never got bad enough for me to leave my hamlet for very long. I paid taxes to both sides and went on planting rice."

In 1954, most of the Viet Minh in Tam's area went North after the Geneva Agreements and Gia Hoi was tranquil again. Three years later, trouble started between the government and the Viet Cong. In the late fifties and early sixties, a number of Loc Chau villagers fled to the safer towns and cities. Most of the villagers were Buddhists, but the majority of those who fled were Catholics; eventually the priests left and returned only periodically to say mass for the Catholics who remained. Many villagers, including a few of Tam's friends—but none of his relatives—joined the Viet Cong. In the late fifties, Tam joined the government Self-Defense Corps for three years, "for fun and to protect my hamlet." He gave it up because it took too much time from his field work.

Tam thinks that some people joined or cooperated with the Viet Cong because of a particular grievance against the government, but that others simply sided with the predominant force as the security situation fluctuated. They joined the government side when the government troops were in the area and seemed able to protect them, and the VC when the government troops weren't around. More wound up with the VC because the VC were a much more constant presence, especially at night. "I was one of the only people to make a conscious choice," Tam says. "I had many reasons for not joining the Viet Cong. I knew that Catholics and Communists could not live together. I found the Viet Cong arguments unconvincing. The VC claimed that life in North Viet Nam was much better than life in the South, but I didn't believe them. If that was true, why did so many people come south in 1954 and 1955 after only a few years under Communism? No one felt the need to leave the South except the Viet Minh. The VC said that in a Communist state everyone was equal and enjoyed the same rights and the same material benefits as everyone else. Personally, I wouldn't like that sort of set-up. Sameness doesn't appeal to me. If I work hard, I will do well. If I don't work, I won't eat. That's as it should be. I also didn't join the Viet Cong because I could never bring myself to terrorize people—to kill even my own relatives. This war is much worse than the last one. The fighting is far more widespread and it's harder to keep out of it and to stay put. People don't know which side to take to feel safe. There are so many families with relatives on both sides. I've seen government hamlet chiefs murdered by Viet Cong guerrillas led by their own nephews. It breaks your heart to see Vietnamese families killing each other like that."

In 1962, Gia Hoi became a strategic hamlet. The peasants in Gia Hoi had heard that the Americans had supplied money and barbed wire for the project. When they had to contribute money for the barbed wire and to work without pay to build a fence around the hamlet, they assumed that the American aid went into the pockets of corrupt officials. The Viet Cong were quiescent for a while. After President Diem's death, VC attacks on the hamlet started again. Two of Tam's relatives who had been in the Self-Defense Corps were kidnapped and murdered by the Viet Cong as a part of their campaign of terrorism in the village. Five of his nephews who had been in the Self-Defense Corps were captured by the VC and have disappeared. In early 1964, when Viet Cong pressure on the hamlet became very great, Tam sent his two oldest sons, aged fifteen and seventeen, to Qui Nhon, the provincial capital of Binh Dinh, and one of the only secure places in the province. He feared they would be drafted by the Viet Cong if they stayed at home. His oldest daughter and her husband, who was just as afraid of being drafted by the VC, also went to Qui Nhon.

By November, 1964, Tam seriously contemplated fleeing his hamlet. He knew that the Viet Cong had it in for him: he'd been in the Self-Defense Corps, he was a Catholic, he wouldn't join them, and he even resisted paying taxes to them. He hesitated for a few months. He couldn't quite face losing everything he had worked so hard for and also the hamlet chief urged him to stay on. One night in mid-February, 1965, while he was still hesitating, the VC attacked Gia Hoi. They wiped out four platoons of popular forces and two platoons of ARVN troops then stationed in the hamlet; some of the soldiers were captured but most, including six of Tam's closest friends, were killed. The hamlet chief was also murdered. On the night of the attack, the Viet Cong came to Tam's house and took him prisoner.

47

They held him in a mountain hideout about seven and a half miles from his hamlet for two months. Rice was scarce and when the shortage became acute, the VC allowed Tam to return to his hamlet. A day or two after he got back, some government planes dropped leaflets over the village. The leaflets said that government airborne troops were soon coming to the area for an operation, and urged the population to stand by if they wanted to follow the troops out of the area. That night, the VC again came to kidnap Tam just a few hours before the government airborne troops reached the hamlet. His wife and children were also taken prisoner and held at a VC base at the foot of the mountain, but they were released in a day; the Viet Cong had presumably decided they wouldn't leave the hamlet alone. When Tam got to the mountain hideout for his second stay, the VC told him he had been tried and sentenced to death. A few days after Tam had been captured, one of his fellow prisoners became very ill. Tam and three other prisoners asked the Viet Cong to let them carry the man down to the plain, where he could get decent food and medical treatment. The VC allowed them to go. Tam isn't sure why the VC released him when they had a rice shortage the first time, or why the VC let the sick man be taken down the mountain the second time. He guesses they like to kill people at a chosen moment and in their own way, rather than have them die of illness or starvation. Shortly before Tam and the other prisoners reached the VC camp at the foot of the mountain with the sick man, they stopped for a rest. Tam broke away from the others and sped off in the direction of his hamlet. The first five and a half miles of the way were through an area under complete VC control; he walked nonchalantly, pretending to be a casual stroller. The last two miles were through contested ground. It took Tam several hours to cover these last two miles, darting from bush to bush, and praying he wouldn't fall into a VC booby trap or be shot at by government troops. He got to Gia Hoi safely and learned that the government airborne troops were still in the vicinity and that his hamlet was temporarily quite secure. He decided he would flee Gia Hoi and go to Qui Nhon, where many of his friends and relatives were already living in refugee camps, whenever the first opportunity presented itself; he didn't discuss the plan with anyone. One morning about ten days later, he found that the road from Gia Hoi to the district capital, nine miles away, had been cleared by a government convoy. He hired three tandem bicycles and three men to help peddle the bicycles. He then told his immediate family that they were going to leave Gia Hoi that afternoon. The news pleased his wife. Tam informed only three other people of his decision—his mother, his mother-in-law, and his younger sister (his father, his father-in-law, and his other younger sister were no longer alive). His younger sister wanted very much to go to Qui Nhon, but she and her husband couldn't bear abandoning their house and the land they had worked for. Tam's mother and mother-in-law wouldn't accompany him because they didn't want to die outside their native hamlet. Tam didn't dare tell anyone else of his imminent departure, not even the airborne troops in the village who might have helped him leave. He suspected that the Army was infiltrated by the Viet Cong and in any case he'd had some nasty experiences with the soldiers. They had often stolen his chickens and coconuts and had stolen the door to his house within

49

the past week. "They made a table out of it," Tam says. "I didn't mind. I was preparing to leave everything behind anyway."

Tam and his family set off in the afternoon, on schedule. His wife and the two youngest children rode on one bicycle, three more children rode on the second bicycle, and Tam rode on the third, carrying a few bundles of clothing. The clothes and seven hundred piasters were all Tam took; he left his rice fields, his house, his furniture, and his cooking utensils. He had no gold and seven hundred piasters was the only money he had. The bicycle caravan met some Viet Cong on the road who asked Tam where he and his family were going. Tam said he had two sons in the government Army in Qui Nhon and that he was traveling there to talk them into deserting and returning home. The Viet Cong, who weren't very strong in the area right after the road-clearing operation, may or may not have believed this lie; at any rate they allowed the family to proceed. Tam and his wife, children, and clothes reached the outskirts of the district capital as night was falling. He paid the bicycle peddlers their fee—one hundred piasters each—and let them go; the family took a Lambretta (thirty piasters, for the seven of them) to the main church of the town. Tam knew a priest there who gave the family dinner. There were already many refugees camping on the church grounds. Tam and his family spent the night on the church floor. They left early the next morning, by bus, for Qui Nhon because Tam felt that even the district capital wasn't very secure. The bus ride cost three hundred and fifty piasters. Tam reached Qui Nhon one afternoon in May, 1965, empty-handed.

Tam and his family went right to the main church in

the city, where they knew a priest who ran several of the many refugee camps in Qui Nhon. The priest gave him sixty-six pounds of rice for his family and one loaf of bread for each child. Fortunately, Tam also received two thousand piasters from the people for whom his two oldest sons had worked in the year and a half they had been in Qui Nhon. For washing dishes, carrying water, and doing many other tasks, the boys had been given room and board, plus wages of fifty piasters a month each, which had been kept for them. Tam used a little of this money to buy salt, *nuoc mam*, and vegetables.

Tam started working immediately. Some of his friends and relatives who had been in Qui Nhon for a while took him out with them to collect firewood in the nearby mountain woods. He figured he could average eighty piasters a day at the most, collecting firewood, and that he and his family couldn't live on that. After ten days of collecting firewood, he found a job as a laborer, which he still has. Tam works for a Vietnamese construction firm, carrying bricks and sand and breaking up stones. He works six days a week (Sundays are for church and for resting) and earns one hundred and fifteen piasters a day. "I would make much more if I worked for an American construction firm," Tam says. "The Americans have many soldiers stationed in Qui Nhon and they are doing a lot of building. Workers for the American firms are hired by Vietnamese. If you want a job, you have to bribe them at least three thousand piasters. I can't afford that amount. If I worked for the Americans, I'd make the same basic pay I do now, but I'd earn several hundred more piasters a week by selling the beer cans and soda bottles the Americans leave around. There's one source of money I haven't yet tapped—I haven't had time to take part in digging up any of the wreckages of the American planes that have crashed in the Qui Nhon area. When a plane crashes, the Americans take away only its engines. Some people I know have made two thousand piasters selling pieces of the wings. My family is living from hand to mouth now. I'm the only rice-winner in the family. The minimum we need for food, firewood, cooking oil, clothes, and school for three of my children is three thousand piasters a month—just about what I'm earning. When someone in the family gets sick, or we have to buy some clothes, we have to cut down on what we eat. That wouldn't be necessary if rice in Qui Nhon were sold at the official price. The rice dealers always say there's no rice available at the official price and I have to buy it on the black market for three times as much."

Tam and his family spent their first night in Qui Nhon at the homes of relatives. On their second day, they moved into one of the reception rooms the priests maintain for new arrivals. The original large refugee camps around the main church were full, but when Tam was walking to the mountains to look for firewood, his first week in the city, he noticed that there were some smaller, newer refugee camps on the outskirts of Qui Nhon and realized there were still some tiny plots of land available. He secured the priest's permission to build a hut on one of the plots. It took him a month to build his hut; when it was finished, he moved into it. He had to buy all the necessary building materials himself, which took the last of his sons' two thousand piasters. Tam's one-room hut measures ten feet by ten feet. Cooking is done in a small area in front of the hut. Three sides of the hut are woven bamboo. The fourth side, which is attached to the wall of the hut next door, is made of paper cartons. The roof is corrugated steel. The only furniture Tam has room for is a hammock and two beds. He bought the hammock and one bed and borrowed the other bed from a nephew. Tam's wife and their three youngest children sleep on one bed; he sleeps on the second bed with the three other children who still live at home. Tam's married daughter and her husband live in their own hut with their first child; Tam's oldest son has joined the popular forces and lives in a garrison. There are about two hundred families in Tam's refugee camp, which is situated on a stretch of treeless, sandy land. There is only one well in the camp, and not a single latrine.

"My former kitchen in Gia Hoi was better than this whole hut," Tam says. "At home, my large brick house had many rooms, filled with furniture. I worked hard in my rice fields, though not as hard as I work here. My cash income was lower, but I was able to save about two thousand piasters a year. I didn't spend one piaster for going to the theater, or to a movie, or for keeping a concubine, and we had our own rice, fish, and vegetables. Here, we have to buy everything. At home, the soil was rich and the vegetation was green. There was lots of water and it was less hot and dusty than Qui Nhon. The worst thing about this camp is the complete lack of sanitation facilities. But we have no complaints, even though our living conditions aren't very good and I have to work harder than I did before. We can eat and sleep in peace without worrying that the VC will make us go out and dig up roads, or take us prisoner. I was terrified when the Viet Cong told me I'd been sentenced to death. When I left my hamlet, all I wanted to do was get away from the Communists. I was quite prepared to accept any hardships. I just wanted to save my skin. After I made my escape, I thought I'd been born a second time."

Before he left Gia Hoi, Tam was afraid the Viet Cong would win the war. Since he has come to Qui Nhon, he no longer thinks the government side will lose, for the simple reason that it is not on its own. He has seen many American and South Korean troops in Qui Nhon and he is impressed by their planes and equipment. Some GIs occasionally come to the refugee camp to play with the children; Tam can't talk to them because he doesn't speak English. "People have told me that the United States is the richest, the strongest, and the biggest country in the world," he says. "And I've heard that there are many peasants in the United States, but their lot is better than ours because the American peasants have machines to help them with their field work." Tam has never heard of Prime Minister Ky. He has heard of Ho Chi Minh. Tam approves of the bombing of North Viet Nam and of Viet Cong targets in South Viet Nam. "We must bomb North Viet Nam much harder and destroy everything up there, so that we can end this war as quickly as possible," he says. "There must be many more airstrikes in South Viet Nam, too, even if some civilians are killed by the bombs. Let whoever is afraid of getting killed flee to secure areas. We must crush the Communists. I'm sure I'd be killed if the Communists won. I'm in favor of invading North Viet Nam because I think that all the people there who hate Communism would join us if we gave them the opportunity. I want to see the country reunified, but that can't be done until we crush the Communists."

Although he now believes in ultimate victory over the

54

Communists, Tam has a few worries. "I'm afraid that the VC will infiltrate this camp," he says. "I think they're trying to do it. The priest here told me there are a million refugees in South Viet Nam, about a hundred thousand in Binh Dinh province alone, and that some of them were leaving their homes because of the bombing and fighting and not because of the Viet Cong. I'm also afraid that the government will uproot us. This camp was built on government land. It seems that the government wants the land back and the priests have their hands full persuading the government to let us stay here. We heard that the government, with American aid, was supposed to help the refugees. It doesn't look that way. But what I worry about most is whether I'll ever see my hamlet again. I've never tried to contact my mother or mother-in-law by mail; it would be futile. I've had word that they are still alive and that the VC came to chew them out after I took off, but they didn't beat them. My mother and mother-in-law are both over eighty. They are too old to beat. I imagine my sister and her husband are having to pay heavy taxes to the Viet Cong and to obey them. I'm sure the VC have taken over my land. I don't miss the social life in my hamlet very much because I don't trust anybody there. I only miss my mother and my mother-in-law and my old way of life. I'd rather return to Gia Hoi than go anywhere in the world. I've never been to Saigon. I don't care to go there. I can't go home now, because I have nothing to go home to. When the war is over, perhaps I'll be able to go home again, but perhaps it won't be possible. I don't like to think that I'll have to live in a refugee camp forever."

»»»» *IV* ««««

>>>>> *D*r. *Tran Ngoc Diep* is a pediatrician by profession, a politician by inclination. Dr. Diep, one of Saigon's many doctor-politicians, is a plump man with gray wavy hair. He is a voluble, non-stop talker who speaks Vietnamese strongly laced with French, perhaps as a result of the French education he received in Hanoi, perhaps as a result of having lived in France for fifteen of the last eighteen years.

Diep was born on April 10, 1918, in Phu Ly, the capital of Ha Nam province, when it was part of the French protectorate of Tonkin. His father was a mandarin who served as a district chief. His grandfather had also been a mandarin and a district chief and his great-grandfather, a senior mandarin, had been the governor of three provinces.

Diep's family was wealthy; his parents always employed a chauffeur, a cook, and several maids and nurses for their many children. Diep was the tenth of twelve children; he had seven sisters and four brothers. Of the five boys, Diep was the one most interested in his father's work. As a young boy, he used to help his father with his paperwork and travel with him on his administrative tours. "My brothers were a bit lazy," Diep says. "Since I was hard-working and pretty intelligent, and spoke good French, my father used to let me help him. I became sort of his private secretary. My father was one of the few honest government officials. He pointed out many instances to me of how other officials took advantage of the low people. Thus, I got to understand the grievances, the aspirations, and the sorry plight of the peasants. That's why I decided from then on to devote my life to politics. Even at the age of ten, I was quite on top of domestic and international developments. I knew about Gandhi's struggle for India's independence, so my father and I had a special relationship."

Diep attended primary school in Phu Ly and then went to secondary school in Hanoi, thirty-five miles away. He attended the Lycée du Protectorat, a well-known school, first as a boarder, later, after his father retired and the family moved to Hanoi, as a day student. Classes were conducted in French; Vietnamese was taught as a foreign language although the students were all Vietnamese. "The school was as strictly organized and as tough as Eton," Diep says. "The French made it difficult because they wanted to hold us down. I passed every examination on my first try." Diep got his first baccalaureate in 1938, his second in 1939. His mother wanted him to become a government official, but his father advised him to take up a profession since the administration was so corrupt. Diep chose medicine and enrolled at the School of Medicine in Hanoi. In August, 1945, when the Viet Minh seized control of Hanoi, Diep's medical studies were interrupted; he continued to work in the hospital where the medical students received their clinical training, and in a rehabilitation center he had set up to help war victims learn a new trade. Diep was married on December 12, 1946, to a girl who was a neighbor of his family in Hanoi. His mother had wanted him to marry a girl from a much richer family, but his parents didn't oppose his marriage. "Our courtship was very smooth," Diep says. "We married out of love and out of mutual respect, too. My wife admired my philanthropic activities." Diep and his wife are both Buddhists. A few days after Diep's marriage, fighting broke out between the Viet Minh and the French in Hanoi. The hospital in which he worked had been taken over by the Viet Minh in August, 1945, and the Viet Minh now moved as much of its equipment as they could out of Hanoi, which was soon in French hands, and into one of the newly created Viet Minh interzones in the countryside. Diep and his wife left Hanoi with the hospital staff and equipment and moved around with them as the war spread during the following months. "During that time, I got to know about the misery and the aspirations of the peasant population, and about the Viet Minh system," Diep says. "I treated wounded Viet Minh soldiers and peasants hurt in the crossfire, so I don't have any feelings of guilt now regarding the citizen's duties to resist the French colonialists." The Viet Minh political commissar assigned to Diep's area tried unsuccessfully to enroll him in the Communist Party. "I knew that under a Communist system people couldn't express their ideas freely," Diep says. "I also didn't like the fact that the Communists insisted on a class struggle to give priority to the proletariat, thus creating a new class at the expense of other classes and creating new injustices. The old injustices were better. Things are even worse today in North Viet

Nam than they are in South Viet Nam." The political commissar was so angry with Diep for not joining the party that he had him transferred to another Viet Minh interzone. Diep was told that he would be under surveillance on the way to his new assignment, but he wasn't escorted and managed to escape into a French-controlled area and from there into Hanoi in December, 1947. "I thought the French were a lesser evil than the Viet Minh because I believed the French would have to leave Viet Nam eventually even if they defeated the Viet Minh," he says. "And anyway, staying with the Viet Minh but refusing to join them meant certain liquidation, so between the certainty of death and the hope of survival I had to choose the French."

In Hanoi, Diep worked at a French hospital, completed his thesis, got his medical degree, opened an office, and practiced medicine for a year. In December, 1948, he left for France; his wife and their first two children joined him in Paris in 1949. "I went to France to continue my medical studies, to widen my knowledge of current international politics, and because I couldn't stand living under French rule in Viet Nam," Diep says. "France had signed a treaty with Emperor Bao Dai, recognizing Viet Nam's sovereignty, in June, 1948. Bao Dai was a French puppet and the treaty was meaningless." Except for three brief visits to Viet Nam before 1954, Diep was out of the country for the next fifteen years.

From 1948 to 1951, Dr. Diep studied in France and traveled around western Europe on a scholarship. He also had some money from the sale of his house and clinic in Hanoi. In 1951, he met a Vietnamese friend then living in Paris, Dr. Trinh Van Luu. At that time, most of the Vietnamese residing in France were either disinterested in politics, pro-Viet Minh, or pro-Bao Dai. Dr. Diep and Dr. Luu thought there was a fourth alternative and launched a political party, the Vietnamese Republican Party, to work for the overthrow of the Bao Dai régime and for real independence for Viet Nam. Diep opened a medical office in Paris in 1951, to finance his political activities. In 1952, Dr. Luu went to the United States. Dr. Diep was left in charge of the party in France. "In 1953, Diem visited me because I was really someone in Paris at the time," Diep says. "We kept in close touch during 1953 and 1954. After Diem was appointed prime minister in 1954, he invited me to cooperate with him. He even asked me to come to Saigon and I did, for a few days. I decided against working with him. At that time I thought Mr. Diem was a good man, but he had to consult his brother, Mr. Nhu, constantly. I saw that Mr. Nhu was running everything and he appeared pretty arrogant. I also realized that many prospective ministers of Mr. Diem's government had no personality, self-respect, or competence, so I declined his offer. I returned to France. In 1955, Mr. Diem asked me twice to come back to cooperate with him. I refused, because I saw he was going to become a dictator. I didn't like the way he got himself elected president. He would have defeated Bao Dai in an honest election, but he rigged the referendum and that was clear proof to me that he wasn't going to respect democratic procedures." Diep and his party, whose name was changed to the Free Democratic Party, since South Viet Nam had become at least nominally a republic under Diem, drifted into opposition against Diem. Dr. Luu returned to South Viet Nam in 1955; in 1960, he was thrown into jail by Diem. Diep then left the party, but

63

continued to oppose the Diem régime. After publishing a white paper denouncing the shortcomings of Diem's government and pointing out how the Communists were exploiting such shortcomings, Dr. Diep flew to the United States and spent two months, December, 1961, and January, 1962, there. "I tried to see President Kennedy and I didn't succeed, but I visited *Time, Newsweek,* the *New York Herald Tribune,* the *Washington Post,* and the AFL-CIO," he says. "I met with many state department officials and senators. I had dinner at Arthur Schlesinger, Jr.'s, house. I tried to point out to everyone that the Vietnamese people wanted a really democratic government instead of Diem. I realized that at that time the American ambassador to South Viet Nam, Frederick Nolting, was in favor of sticking with Diem, so I didn't see any immediate prospect for a change in the political scene in Viet Nam. After presenting my viewpoint to American personalities, I went back to Paris. Moreover, the Laotian question was a burning one and I wanted to follow its development closely." Dr. Diep had several dinners with Prince Souvanna Phouma and recommended him to an American official of his acquaintance as a staunch anti-Communist. "My own opinion is that it's owing to my recommendation that Mr. Phouma became prime minister of Laos," Diep says.

In 1962, Dr. Diep went to Cambodia, where he told Cambodia's ruler, Prince Sihanouk, that it was a mistake for him to woo the Communists. He also founded an anti-Diem organization called the National Council of the Vietnamese Revolution with Colonel Nguyen Chanh Thi, who had been living in exile in Cambodia since commanding the unsuccessful November, 1960, paratroopers' coup against Diem.

Diep flew to Tokyo and to the United States to announce the Council's formation and then returned to France.

Between January and October, 1963, Diep lived in Paris, but arranged to have a few harmless bombs set off in various parts of Saigon; when the bombs exploded, they scattered hundreds of tiny mimeographed leaflets, demanding Diem's overthrow and carrying the name of the Council and of Dr. Diep. Diep was planning other anti-Diem ploys from Paris when the coup against Diem occurred; Diep returned to Saigon in December, 1963.

To "learn about the political awareness of the peasants and their current plight, grievances, and aspirations," Diep toured South Viet Nam from February to May, 1964, by bus and plane. "I realized that even people in remote areas had heard about my activities abroad and my activities against Mr. Diem from press and radio reports," he says. "I got out of a bus in one city, where I didn't know anyone, and a man came up to me and asked if I was Dr. Diep. I realized I was very popular. That tour was the happiest time of my life."

In June, 1964, Diep founded the Movement of Struggle for the People's Rights, to work for representative government and against military rule. In November, 1964, he started a daily newspaper called *To Win*. Its line was also anti-military rule and pro-democracy. He shut it down after seven days because of heavy censorship and left Saigon for a second tour of the countryside, which lasted three weeks. Upon his return, he published his paper again on December 19th. On December 20th, he was picked up by the agents of Lieutenant General Nguyen Khanh, who was then in power. He was taken by military plane to jail in Kontum, a province in the central highlands, where he spent three weeks in confinement with members of the High National Council, a representative body Khanh had just disbanded. The food wasn't much, but the prisoners weren't too badly treated. "It was a good experience," Diep says. "It was my first time in jail." He spent his time reading, and he also wrote a poem:

> I am staying in Kontum at the beginning of the year
> While tigers and wolves are terrorizing the population.
> I've forgotten all my misfortunes because I've been
>   exclusively concerned with the nation's affairs,
> But occasionally I do miss my family.
> In spite of difficulties, I never allow myself to
>   be down-hearted
> Or to bow under pressure.
> I am confident of final victory;
> And then we will be able to do all kinds of good
>   things for the people.

"The tigers and wolves are General Khanh and all the other generals and their henchmen," Diep says. He now has the poem embroidered in large gold letters on a red cloth background and mounted on a stand in his roomy, well-staffed apartment in the center of Saigon.

After his release from jail, Diep was flown back to Saigon by military plane on January 10th. His paper had been closed down while he was in Kontum; he reopened it on April 15th; it was closed down by Marshal Ky on July 4th, two weeks after Ky took power. Since then, Diep has been busy writing a pamphlet called "A Policy for Winning Victory

Over the Communists in Viet Nam," which he plans to circulate when it is finished.

In August, 1965, Diep brought his six children, whose ages range from nine to eighteen, to Saigon. The two oldest had been born in North Viet Nam, the four youngest in France. This was the first time any of the children had been to South Viet Nam. They attended French schools in Paris and now attend French government-sponsored schools in Saigon. Diep is very critical of South Vietnamese generals whose children are now studying in French schools in France. In May, 1965, Diep set up a pediatric clinic in Saigon, and he says he works at it six days a week, but he often takes days off to talk to foreign journalists because he feels the need to better inform the American public. "I spoke quite good English after my two trips to the States," he says. "I've forgotten so much of it now." He sometimes talks for nine hours at a stretch, in a mixture of French and Vietnamese.

Dr. Diep was happy when the Diem régime was overthrown, but he soon had misgivings about the parade of governments that followed Diem's. "The basic mistakes of Mr. Diem's régime are in force to this day, except that arbitrary arrest no longer prevails," Diep says. "Freedom of speech still doesn't exist, political activities are still banned, and corruption is more rampant than ever. None of the governments since Diem have been acceptable to me. The leaders have all tolerated so much corruption that the peasants have continued to suffer from social injustices, oppression, and exploitation. The peasants still have no rights to defend themselves and they are at the mercy of corrupt government officials. Before Marshal Ky became prime minister, he promised to shoot the country's twenty-eight leading rice dealers, one by one, until the price of rice went down or the last dealer was dead. Well, Marshal Ky has been in office for a long, long time, the rice price is still artificially high, and all the leading rice dealers are very much alive. Ky also promised to shoot the war profiteers. All he did was shoot one Chinese businessman and a few common criminals; some of them had been languishing in jail for five years." Another thing Diep holds against all the post-Diem régimes is their tolerance and encouragement of anti-Americanism in South Viet Nam. "The leaders are afraid of being called valets of the Americans so they make statements thanking for help from the 'free world' instead of help from the United States," Diep says. "North Viet Nam is far more candid about Chinese aid than South Viet Nam is about American aid. The South Vietnamese leaders won't permit a word of criticism against themselves, but they let students in South Viet Nam put out magazines carrying Viet Cong propaganda against the war and against the American presence here. The South Vietnamese leaders are worried about their country's sovereignty. Sovereignty—the idea is laughable when you've got three hundred thousand foreign troops on your soil. The United States should be in overt control here. Americans shouldn't worry about world opinion. The peasants would be glad to have Americans running their districts and provinces instead of corrupt Vietnamese colonels. Americans are much more honest than Vietnamese. If Americans were in charge, all of the American aid might reach the peasants instead of feathering the nests of corrupt government officials. The peasants know that Vietnamese officials have never cared about their welfare. It's the American soldiers who are sponsoring orphanages and giving medical treatment to the peasants in the countryside. The United States has only one foreign policy—to defend free nations against Communist aggression—and I agree with this policy. History has taught us that appeasement doesn't work. The Americans are doing only one thing wrong as far as the war in South Viet Nam is concerned. They talk too much about unconditional negotiations. No one in South Viet Nam who isn't pro-VC favors such negotiations. We know that the only negotiations the Communists would enter into would be the kind that would enable them to take over the country. The United States should stop talking about negotiations. If we want to have real peace in South Viet Nam, we have to go on with the war and win it. People who advise peace at all costs are just false sentimentalists. I reject the idea of negotiations. I may appear inhuman, but that's not so. I insist on winning the war to save future lives. If we accept peace under Communist rule, many thousands of people in South Viet Nam will be sentenced to death by Communist People's Tribunals, as they were in North Viet Nam when the Communists took over. And if the Communists get South Viet Nam, they will then proceed further, to Cambodia and Thailand. People in South Viet Nam will be sent to fight for the Communists in those countries, just as North Vietnamese were sent to Laos to help the Pathet Lao. Many of them lost their lives. We must continue to bomb North Viet Nam and Viet Cong targets in the south. From all I understand, the bombing is really weakening the Communists. I know that we sometimes kill women and children when we bomb villages, but mistakes in war are inevitable and people are ready to forgive such mistakes. Viet Nam has been at war in previous centuries for much longer than twenty years at a time. I don't worry too much about this war in perspective. What we should do is make the most of this war, for the benefit of future generations. The Communists in North Viet Nam are geared up to suffer more, in order to enhance the American public's discontent with the war. Many people in America are awed by the image of the Viet Cong and Ho Chi Minh. They shouldn't be. Actually, Ho Chi Minh is a great failure. He did defeat the French, but he's not a national hero. In the last ten years, he hasn't thought of his country's interests, but only of establishing Communism in Viet Nam. As a result of his Communist views, North Viet Nam is a shabby country, South Viet Nam is at war, and all the Vietnamese people have been suffering. All Vietnamese are eager for reunification, just as the Germans are, but since reunification is impossible right now, we should work toward making South Viet Nam a country like West Germany. North Viet Nam is already like East Germany. If things in South Viet Nam were so good that a barrier had to be set up between the two countries and the North Vietnamese risked their lives to come down here to live, that would be a big achievement. The United States can't afford to abandon South Viet Nam and victory is certain if the Americans stay, but we can't really win the war with the present government. We have to have a truly representative, democratic, honest, sincere government before we can induce the peasants and the Viet Cong to take our side. Only a true democracy can win over the Communists. The Communists are to blame for starting the war, but the Diem régime was also at fault. When given a choice between the Communists and the corrupt, dictatorial Diem régime, many peasants chose

Communism. There's a lesson to be learned from Diem's having been kept in office too long, with the help of the Americans. I think we should set a time limit for a government to prove its worth. Prime Minister Ky isn't very popular or very effective. He ought to go, and anyway I think we should let the military take care of the war and the civilians take care of the administration. On the military plane, we don't have as much to do as we had before; we have to concentrate more on the political field. Generals aren't politicians. Of course I'd like to take up responsibility. It's useless to have good ideas and not be able to carry them out. If I get power, I have a clean record. I didn't work with the French or with Diem. I've always been against neutralism and Communism. I've always been against everything except democracy."

》》》》》 *V* 《《《《《

>>>>> *A* mi *Yoh* is a montagnard. She belongs
to the Rhade tribe. The montagnards (a term derived from
the French *tribus montagnards*) are the primitive tribesmen who live in the mountainous areas of North and South
Viet Nam, Cambodia, and Laos. There are an estimated
seven hundred thousand to a million montagnards in South
Viet Nam's central highlands, a sparsely populated region
that covers two thirds of the country—all but the Mekong
delta and the narrow central coastal plains.

The montagnards are Vietnamese only by political fiat;
ethnically and linguistically they fall into two non-Vietnam-
ese groups, the Malayo-Polynesian and the Mon-Khmer.
Opinions vary as to their geographic origins, but the montagnards are believed to have migrated to the Indo-Chinese
peninsula thousands of years ago and to have been its original inhabitants. They apparently once lived in the fertile
rice deltas of South Viet Nam's lowlands and were forced
into the rugged highlands by aggressive newcomers, such as
the Vietnamese, when they pushed down from China along
the coast.

There are about a dozen major montagnard tribes and perhaps sixty minor ones in South Viet Nam. Some of the smallest and most primitive tribes still eat human flesh, practice slavery, and take one bath a year; they live in remote regions and have had little contact with the rest of the world. The Rhade tribe is considered the most sophisticated and is one of the three or four largest tribes numerically, with approximately one hundred and twenty thousand members. The Rhade have had more contact with outsiders than most other tribes. They are centered around Ban Me Thuot, a city one hundred and sixty miles north of Saigon, on the relatively accessible Darlac plateau. The language of the Rhade is of Malayo-Polynesian origin and a Polynesian influence is evident in their physical characteristics. Ami Yoh is a handsome woman. She has a broad nose, good teeth, prominent cheekbones, and straight black hair, worn in a small bun. The lightness of her skin is a sign of beauty to the montagnards, many of whom have dark brown complexions. Her voice and manner are firm. She wears a traditional montagnard black ankle-length wraparound skirt, a western-style black-and-white checked sleeveless blouse, and yellow rubber sandals. When Ami Yoh was a child, the men in her village wore loincloths, the women skirts. "The women wore blouses only if they felt like it and if they wanted to take the trouble to put them on," she says. "Shirts were optional for the men, too." In recent years, the Vietnamese government and western missionaries have dissuaded the montagnard women from going bare-breasted, although many still do. The Rhade men who have been exposed to American soldiers have developed a spontaneous fondness for GI T-shirts.

Ami Yoh was born in 1934 in Buon Jak Jin, a montagnard village fifteen miles from Ban Me Thuot, the capital of the highland province of Darlac. In the nineteen-thirties, Ban Me Thuot was a small trading center and plantation town; it is now a city of fifty thousand. Buon Jak Jin's appearance has scarcely changed since Ami Yoh's childhood. It is located in a cleared area of the rain forest, near a river, two miles from the next closest montagnard village. It consists of thirty longhouses, arranged in parallel rows, constructed entirely of wood and bamboo, with thatched roofs. The longhouses are built on stilts about five feet off the ground; notched logs serve as staircases. Ami Yoh does not think much of the Vietnamese and some other tribes who build their houses at ground level with dirt floors. "Houses on stilts can be swept cleaner and they stay drier when the heavy rains fall from the sky," she says. "They also protect you from tigers and other wild beasts."

The size of a longhouse (usually fifty to one hundred feet long, and about twenty feet wide) is determined by the number (usually fifteen to fifty people) and the wealth of its residents. Ami Yoh was the youngest of her parents' six surviving children. When she was a girl, she lived in a longhouse one hundred feet long with her parents, several maternal aunts, their husbands and children, her three older brothers, and her two older sisters. The Rhade are matrilinear and matrilocal—as time went by, Ami Yoh's brothers and male cousins married and moved into the longhouses of their wives' families, and her sisters and female cousins married and brought their husbands to live with them. "One of my sisters married a Rhade serving in the French Army who could read and write," Ami Yoh says. "He figured out

77

my age for me." The population of the longhouse remained fairly constant, at about thirty-five.

After sidling up a notched log, one arrives at the front porch of the longhouse (used for rice-pounding and gossiping, as is the back porch) and then enters the communal meeting room, where guests are received, weapons and tools are stored, ceremonies are held, and such valued ceremonial items as wine jugs, gongs, and a large drum are kept. Behind the communal room, along one side of the longhouse, are partitioned sleeping compartments for the individual families. Opposite each compartment on the corridor that runs the length of the longhouse are the separate family rice pots and cooking fires. "My cousins and I quarreled about whose mother served better food and more of it," Ami Yoh says. In theory, the smoke from the cooking fires is blown out of the longhouse's windows by the prevailing winds; in practice, the longhouse is a very smoky place. Buon Jak Jin had no such amenities as electricity or sanitary facilities when Ami Yoh was a child, and has none today. A few longhouses now boast such dubious improvements as corrugated iron roofs, which make them far hotter than those covered by thatched roofs.

Ami Yoh had a carefree childhood. She did not go to school. In the nineteen-thirties and early forties, there were some Rhade schools run by the French in the principal towns in the highlands, but very few children from the villages attended them. Until she was eight, Ami Yoh spent her time playing and taking dips in the river. Then she began to do some household chores—she swept the house, carried water and firewood, husked rice, and helped care for the family horse, buffalos, pigs, and chickens. The Rhade planted cotton and spun thread from it, and Ami Yoh learned how to weave and dye cloth. She also looked after her sisters' children while her sisters were at work in the rice fields. The Rhade grow dry rice and practice the wasteful and destructive slash-and-burn method of agriculture, which requires an abundance of land. To obtain rice fields, they cut down and then burn the trees and brush in a given spot. The ashes produced serve as fertilizer and make the soil rich enough for three or four years of crops. When the soil is depleted, the field is abandoned (it then returns to its wild state, is revitalized by the forest growth, and is recultivated a few years later) and the process is repeated elsewhere. Ami Yoh ate quite well as a child. Dry rice was the staple food. The Rhade also ate the assorted vegetables and fruit they grew in small gardens or gathered from the forest, as well as fish, wild game they trapped or killed with their crossbows and arrows, and rats, lizards, and snakes. For some reason, Ami Yoh gets sick nowadays if she eats dog or monkey meat, but she still considers lizard salad a great delicacy. The Rhade generally reserve domestic animals for ritual sacrifices and eat them only on ceremonial occasions. They often run out of rice in the months immediately preceding the annual rice harvest. "Over half the harvest is used to make rice wine," Ami Yoh says. A common Rhade greeting is "Let's get drunk together." The Rhade get happy when they drink and think the animistic spirits they worship become as happy as they do.

The Rhade worship a densely-populated pantheon of spirits, both good and evil, which they believe inhabit the sky and the earth, the rivers and the forests, and innumerable other animate and inanimate objects. Since they are convinced that the spirits affect their lives—evil or angry spirits can cause anything from a petty annoyance to a major disaster, such as crop failure or a smallpox epidemic— the Rhade spend most of their time trying to remain on friendly terms with these spirits. Omens and dreams are considered pertinent messages from benign spirits. If a crow lands on a longhouse while it is being built, the structure must be abandoned or the future inhabitants will suffer bad luck. A dream about an accident is a warning to stay at home and avoid an inevitable mishap.

The Rhade feel that the best way to appease evil spirits and to keep the favor of good spirits is to offer them sacrifices. There are prescribed sacrifices for major events in the agricultural cycle (the planting and the harvest) and in the life cycle (birth, marriage, and death). Special sacrifices are necessary when someone has violated a village taboo, such as incest, and thus offended the spirits. When a Rhade is ill, a sorcerer must be called in to determine the spirit responsible for the illness and the kind of sacrifice required to placate it and thus cure the afflicted person. "Sacrifices usually depend on the wealth of the sick person and his family," Ami Yoh says. They usually begin with rice wine and a chicken or two. If the illness is not cured, a pig or a goat is sacrificed. If these sacrifices, in conjunction with the herb medicines the spirits permit the sorcerer to administer, fail, one or more buffalos are sacrificed. If this is unsuccessful, the sorcerer, a powerful person in the village who collects high fees for his services, usually escapes responsibility by explaining to the sick man's family that the spirits will not settle for anything less than the man's body and that he will therefore never recover. In the early nineteen-forties, some western missionaries who lived in Ban Me Thuot came to Buon Jak Jin and other Rhade villages and attempted to convert the montagnards to Christianity. The missionaries are still working with the various tribes and making some converts, but to this day the overwhelming majority of montagnards are animists.

Buon Jak Jin is a rather self-contained village. The Rhade have never achieved political unity on a tribal level and each village governs itself. While Ami Yoh was growing up, the men and boys in her village went hunting or walked into Ban Me Thuot to trade rice and firewood for beads, mirrors, jars, and gongs. The French and Vietnamese traders found the Rhade about as shrewd as the Dutch West India Company found the American Indians who sold them the island of Manhattan for twenty-four dollars worth of trinkets. The jars and gongs had little intrinsic value, but the Rhade required them for their ceremonies and thus they became a measure of wealth. The boys occasionally went courting in other villages, but young girls like Ami Yoh generally stayed at home. Except for the missionaries and some Rhade from neighboring villages who called on their relatives once in a while, few outsiders came to Buon Jak Jin during Ami Yoh's childhood. Ami Yoh remembers how surprised she was when two hunters from another tribe, the M'nong, turned up in her village one day. "I was five or six years old and when I saw the M'nong and heard them talking, I realized for the first time that there were people in the world who weren't Rhade, and that there were other languages besides ours," she says. When Ami Yoh was ten, a Frenchman started a coffee plantation near Buon Jak Jin and hired a Vietnamese to design and supervise the building of his house. The Vietnamese architect—the first Vietnamese Ami Yoh had ever seen—occasionally passed the village on his way to and from Ban Me Thuot. "I couldn't get over his slanted eyes and the funny way he walked," she says. "He seemed even more peculiar looking to me than that French coffee planter."

When the French colonized Viet Nam in the late nineteenth century, they attempted to pacify the montagnards. Pacification was a slow, seesaw process, more successful with some tribes than with others. The Rhade initially resisted the entrance of the French into the highlands, murdering a number of missionaries and soldiers. By the first quarter of the twentieth century, the Rhade were cooperating with the French and serving in the colonial Army, and were helping the French pacify other more bellicose tribes, which did not submit until the late nineteen-thirties.

In 1893, the highland area officially became part of the French protectorate of Annam, and the French decided to administer the highlands separately from the rest of Viet Nam. The French exploited the economic resources of the highlands; they established tea, rubber, coffee, and tobacco plantations and practically excluded Vietnamese from the area. Only a few Vietnamese, mostly traders and servants for the French planters and administrators (the montagnards made miserable cooks) were granted permits to come to the highlands. In 1940, there were only one hundred and twenty-three Vietnamese in Ban Me Thuot. The montagnards considered this policy of denying the Vietnamese entry into the highlands, which obviously benefited the French, also beneficial to themselves. Before the French takeover of the country, conflict between the montagnards and the Vietnamese had been kept to a minimum, since the Vietnamese never really wanted to inhabit the highlands and were primarily concerned with keeping the montagnards up there and out of the fertile lowlands, but there had long been antipathy between the two groups. The Vietnamese had extracted an annual tribute from the montagnards and had controlled and monopolized trade with the tribes, cheating them at every opportunity and treating them with scorn. They had not bothered to conceal the fact that they had absorbed Chinese civilization and considered themselves highly refined, and that they looked down upon the montagnards as barbarians. "The Vietnamese have always called the montagnards *moi*," Ami Yoh says. "*Moi* means savages. It's as if they think we're animals." In general, the montagnards and the French got along better than the montagnards and the Vietnamese ever had.

The montagnards were subject to few restrictions under the French. In the early part of the twentieth century, several capable French administrators had roads built and created an administration for the highlands, employing montagnards in many posts, and developed a written form of the Rhade language (many tribes still have no written language). The French respected Rhade custom-law. They recorded and codified these laws and created a tribal court system; they felt that the alternative, French law, would have been far too disruptive for the montagnards. The Rhade didn't like to contribute labor to the building of roads and the rubber boom brought a rush for plantations in the highlands. In the nineteen-twenties, French plantations began to encroach on tribal land, but the French always asked for the land they wanted and negotiated politely for it. The prices they paid, insignificant as they were to the French, were important to the Rhade. "Sometimes the French paid more than the asking price for land if a village was poor," Ami Yoh says. "They would pay sixty buffalos instead of fifty. They were willing to spend two weeks on a transaction that could have been completed in a day. The French knew the art of diplomacy." Ami Yoh and many other montagnards now tend to idealize life in the French days, especially in the light of what followed.

Ami Yoh's childhood ended in 1946, when she was twelve years old. That year, a young man of eighteen returned to Buon Jak Jin, his native village. His mother and father had divorced some years previously, and his mother lived in Ban Me Thuot; he came to the village to visit some maternal relatives. He had spent the last few years traveling around the highlands with his father, a soldier in the French colonial Army, who had recently died. The young man had attended French primary and then secondary schools in the various cities where his father had been posted, most recently in Da Lat, the largest city in the highlands. He had a few weeks of vacation before he was to take his examinations. He met Ami Yoh soon after his arrival in Buon Jak Jin. They fell in love and decided they wanted to be married. "I was big for my age," Ami Yoh says. Not long before the marriage was to take place, Ami Yoh's father became ill. Her mother sacrificed all of the family's domestic animals and rice wine to the spirits. Her father died anyway. Ami Yoh's mother couldn't afford to stage an elaborate wedding feast, so the couple simply exchanged bracelets and sipped a little rice wine through a common reed. Soon after the wedding, Ami Yoh's husband returned to Da Lat for his examinations. He passed them and accepted a job in Ban Me Thuot with the French provincial administration. Ami Yoh and her husband were driven into Ban Me Thuot by a Protestant missionary couple. It was Ami Yoh's first ride in an automobile and her first trip to Ban Me Thuot, where she went to live in a longhouse near the center of town. "I was so awed by the cars and all the wonders of Ban Me Thuot that I could hardly tear myself away from my front porch to cook my husband's rice," she says. During their first year in Ban Me Thuot, Ami Yoh and her husband began going to the church the missionaries had established there. In 1947, they were both converted to Christianity. In 1949, her husband felt the call to be a pastor, resigned from his job, and attended the Missionary Bible School in Ban Me Thuot. After some months of classes, he was sent out to Rhade villages to preach, then returned to the Bible School for additional training. In 1950, he became a pastor.

In their twenty years of married life, Ami Yoh has had seven children. Two girls and four boys are alive; one boy died of illness. "When he was six, he suddenly became feverish," Ami Yoh says. "Then something in his stomach seemed to move and he would jump and run just like a mad dog. He died very quickly. God has been good to us. Many of my friends have lost five or six out of seven children." Ami Yoh's oldest child, a boy named Y'Yoh, born in 1950, is responsible for the names by which she and her husband have been known for the last sixteen years. Ami Yoh's name at birth was H'Kloin (H' is the female Rhade prefix); her husband's name was Y'Gor (Y' is the male Rhade prefix). Upon the birth of a Rhade couple's first child, the new parents become known as Ami (the mother of) and Ama (the father of) that child. Ami and Ama Yoh's second child, a daughter named H'Be, was born in 1952. Their four other living children range in age from three to twelve. The children take their mother's family name, K'sor, rather than their father's, Niehraa.

From 1950 to 1962, Ama Yoh was a pastor in various Rhade villages in Darlac province. He converted many Rhade to Christianity. Separating the tribespeople from their belief in animistic spirits freed them from their constant fears, taboos, and sacrifices. Rhade who become Christians give up drinking alcohol; a diet without rice wine is healthier and saves them time. "Many Rhade often lie around drunk for three whole days," Ami Yoh says. After her marriage, Ami Yoh learned to read Rhade (she still doesn't read or speak Vietnamese, or any other language) and she helped her husband in his work by conducting Bible classes. As the Second Indo-China War intensified in the highlands, life in the more remote villages became very dangerous for Ami and Ama Yoh. Christians were a particular target of the Viet Cong, who found them much harder to subvert, and the VC have murdered several Rhade pastors. Four years ago, Ami and Ama Yoh moved back to Ban Me Thuot, where Ama Yoh works as a clerk.

Ami and Ama Yoh live with five of their six children (Y'Yoh no longer lives at home) and Ami Yoh's aged mother in a three-room wooden house. The house has electricity, cement floors, several beds, a few other pieces of furniture, and huge cobwebs on the beams. "I wouldn't live at ground level with dirt floors, but if I have cement floors that's all right," Ami Yoh says. The cobwebs don't strike Ami Yoh as dirty, and it has never occurred to her to get

86

rid of them. Dogs and chickens, as well as the lizards that go into Ami Yoh's salads, abound in the earth yard around the house.

Ami Yoh spends her time cooking, taking care of her children, conducting Bible classes, and going to market. She and her mother buy cotton thread in Ban Me Thuot and weave it into colorful montagnard cloth. "The American soldiers buy a lot of it," she says. "I have no idea what they do with it." Ami Yoh's mother also helps her with her chores. "It is the Rhade custom for a mother to live with her youngest daughter," she says. "If the youngest daughter isn't alive, a mother lives with the next youngest daughter. Parents would be in difficult straits if they had no daughter to live with in their old age. They would have to live alone. They wouldn't move in with their sons and daughters-in-law. That would be like eating someone else's rice." Ama Yoh earns three thousand piasters a month as a clerk and he earns a little extra by acting as a middleman for illiterate Rhade villagers peddling coffee and other items to shopkeepers in town. Ami and Ama Yoh need all the money they can manage to earn, because of the high cost of living in Ban Me Thuot. Their four oldest children have attended school and they hope to be able to afford to send the two youngest when they are of school age.

Ami Yoh used to visit her relatives in Buon Jak Jin every few months, but she has not gone home for over a year, as it is too dangerous. "There is too much war," she says. She does not regret living in a city rather than in a village. "I actually prefer an individual house to a longhouse," she says. "There's much less quarreling when everyone isn't living under the same roof. There are also more opportunities for children in the city. There is now a primary school in Buon Jak Jin, though it only goes up to the third year. But what good are improvements like schools and iron roofs in the midst of what's going on? The war has made the villages such trying places. One of my sisters still lives in our native village. She is so afraid of the Viet Cong that she can hardly sleep at night. In the daytime, she and her husband are afraid to go to the rice fields, for fear planes will spot them and mistake them for Viet Cong. My sister often comes to my house to spend the night. She and her husband would move into Ban Me Thuot if they could, but there are already too many Rhade refugees here, and they wouldn't be able to earn a living. The last twenty years have completely disrupted the traditional montagnard way of life."

In 1945, when the Japanese disarmed the French colonial Army and imprisoned all the French civilians in Viet Nam, the Viet Minh took advantage of the French absence to move into the highlands. After the French returned, the First Indo-China War broke out. The majority of the Rhade fought with the French; some other tribes fought with the Viet Minh. The main roads on which French convoys traveled were often ambushed, but there was not much prolonged fighting in the central highlands and most of the villages were fairly peaceful. Viet Minh propaganda agents proselytized among the montagnards. They made much of the fact that the French, a white people whom the Rhade had come to regard as superior, had been overpowered by an Asian people, the Japanese. The Viet Minh also told the Rhade that the French were encroaching on their land, that they had paid them lower prices for their land than they paid to Vietnamese in the rice deltas, and that they had abused them in other ways. After the partition of the country in 1954, the Viet Minh took several thousand Rhade and other tribesmen to North Viet Nam and left behind a number of underground agents, who lived quietly in tribal villages.

In 1955, the Diem government took over the administration of the highlands and abolished its separate status. Diem set out to assimilate the montagnards into Vietnamese society. When the Second Indo-China War got under way, the central highlands assumed great strategic importance, and the allegiance of the montagnards, the majority of the population there, became invaluable. The infiltration routes from North Viet Nam to the central coast and to the southern portion of South Viet Nam cross the highlands. The montagnards were indispensable to the Viet Cong as guides (since they knew the trails through the rain forest), as porters to carry supplies, and as gatherers of intelligence on the location of government troops.

One of Diem's policies was to move large numbers of Vietnamese into the highlands from the overpopulated coastal regions. Some of the settlers came to the highlands willingly, lured by the promise of plentiful land, but most were made to migrate to the new Land Development Centers against their will. Since only Buddhist hamlets were forcibly moved, whole communities on the central coast converted to Catholicism so they could stay put. The sudden influx of Vietnamese infuriated the montagnards. The Rhade believed they owned all the land in the tribal area, and considered the new settlers trespassers on their land. They were not asked for their land or paid for it, and were no longer even legally allowed to own land themselves. "We protested, but the Vietnamese said they'd thrown out the French and were now our lords and masters," Ami Yoh says. "They told us we had no one else to depend on any more, so we'd have to depend on them." The new settlers killed off much of the game, fished out many streams, and bulldozed sacred montagnard graveyards. Some montagnards were forced into new villages close to Land Development Centers, so that they could supposedly benefit from contact with the superior Vietnamese culture. The montagnards felt that this resettlement program was just another Vietnamese conspiracy to seize their land. They disliked living far from their rice fields and their familiar spirits.

As part of his policy of assimilation, Diem abolished the tribal courts and made the montagnards subject to Vietnamese law, a foreign legal system that did not take into account tribal cultural patterns and values. He no longer permitted montagnard schools to be taught in Rhade and other dialects, as they had been in the French days. The Vietnamese language became compulsory. "H'Be has never studied in any language except Vietnamese," Ami Yoh says. "We've taught her to write in Rhade at home, but it's much easier for her to write in Vietnamese. She misspells Rhade words." When the government soldiers went through montagnard villages on military operations, they raped tribal women, trampled on montagnard rice fields, and helped themselves to whatever struck their fancy. In cities like Ban Me Thuot, Vietnamese have forced the montagnards to give up their longhouses in desirable locations and to build their homes elsewhere. The Rhade felt that the Vietnamese merchants who moved into the highlands in droves after 1955 dealt unfairly with them. The montagnards who brought goods for sale to Ban Me Thuot from their villages were stopped at checkpoints just outside the city limits by Vietnamese soldiers and police, and were robbed of much of what they were carrying. Those who succeeded in getting their goods to market were cheated. "When I bring a chicken to the market to sell, the Vietnamese pay me only half the price they're paying Vietnamese," Ami Yoh says. "They say the montagnards are too ignorant to realize this. We're not. I deal with Chinese shopkeepers as much as possible. They treat us slightly more fairly than the Vietnamese do." The montagnards objected to other discriminatory practices of the Vietnamese. They were given the filthiest beds in the hospitals, where their sick were neglected and uncared for. They were allotted a tiny quota of available places in schools, and much less than their share of government price-controlled rice than the Vietnamese. "We're forced to buy most of our rice on the black market," Ami Yoh says. "That's hard on our budget."

Another major complaint the montagnards have is the contemptuous attitude of the Vietnamese toward them. Although Diem officially banned the word "*moi*" and all Vietnamese officials in the highlands have been instructed to address the montagnards as "highland compatriots," most continue to call the montagnards "*moi*." Even those who don't use the word maintain their customary disdainful attitude to the tribespeople. "Y'Yoh was one of the first Rhade children to get through an all-Vietnamese primary school," Ami Yoh says. "He entered a Vietnamese secondary school. He was the only Rhade in his class. His Vietnamese schoolmates continually threatened to beat him up and were so unkind to him that he couldn't concentrate on his work.

He dropped out of the school after the first year." H'Be is now in her first year of secondary school. There are a few other Rhade students in her class, so it is easier for her; she has friends to support her. "The Rhade and the Vietnamese in H'Be's school quarrel constantly," Ami Yoh says. "The Vietnamese students always mock the Rhade. They laugh at their clothes, their physical appearance, and their poverty. I'm glad H'Be has no intention of marrying a Vietnamese, because I would be terribly opposed to that. It would be worse than having her marry a Rhade unbeliever. Many Vietnamese men have married tribal girls. Before the marriage, they behave politely and promise them all sorts of nice things. Afterwards, they treat them like dirt. It's better for a Rhade to marry a Rhade." The Rhade respond to the haughty attitude of the Vietnamese with deep suspicion. They question every Vietnamese motive and action and always assume the worst. One night not long ago, eight of Ami Yoh's chickens vanished. There are many Rhade in Ban Me Thuot, but Ami Yoh is sure the Vietnamese are responsible for the chickens' disappearance. "Lots of Vietnamese children walk around my neighborhood," she says. "They say they're just walking around, but I know they're keeping their eyes open looking for good things to steal."

In 1958, montagnard discontent coalesced into a movement aimed at achieving autonomy for the tribes. The movement was called Ba-Ja-Rha-Ko, a series of abbreviations for the names of four of the major tribes—the Bahnar, the Jarai, the Rhade, and the Koho. The movement was led by Y'Bham Enuol, a French-educated Rhade and a former civil servant in the colonial administration. The other members of the committee were French-trained montagnard administrators, officers in the colonial Army, or teachers who had been downgraded as a result of the Vietnamese takeover of the highlands. The concept of autonomous status for South Viet Nam's montagnards had antecedents in the First Indo-China War. Both the Viet Minh and the French, for their own opposing ends, had attempted to win the support of the tribesmen by playing on their traditional distrust of and enmity for the Vietnamese. They found that autonomy had a natural appeal to the montagnards. The Ba-Ja-Rha-Ko demanded an autonomous status for the tribes within the Republic of Viet Nam, and the right of the tribes to fly their own flag. The Diem government responded by jailing a number of the principal leaders. Another, Y'Bih Aleo, a Rhade, went into hiding and later joined the South Viet Nam National Liberation Front, the political apparatus of the Viet Cong. He is now listed as a vice president of the Front and its principal representative of the highland tribes. Most of those arrested were released in 1962 and merely kept under surveillance, but others, including Y'Bham and Paul Nur, a Bahnar, remained in prison until after the Diem régime was overthrown in the coup d'état of November, 1963.

The friction between the montagnards and the Vietnamese government played into the hands of the Viet Cong. The Viet Minh cadres who had remained in the highlands after the First Indo-China War became active in 1958, and that year tribesmen who had gone to North Viet Nam and had been trained in propaganda work and guerrilla warfare there, began to infiltrate into the South. When Rhade Viet Cong cadres came to Rhade villages, they were easily accepted, since they were of the same tribe. They were usually accompanied by Vietnamese Communist agents, who gained the confidence of the villagers by participating in communal activities and by complying with Rhade customs. They adopted Rhade dress, filed their teeth as the tribespeople did, spoke the Rhade language, and in many instances took Rhade brides. The South Vietnamese government has never had any cadres that are dedicated enough to spend years living in montagnard villages. "It's not easy to find a Vietnamese on the government side who even speaks Rhade," Ami Yoh says. The Viet Cong cadres exploited every mistake made by the South Vietnamese government and its soldiers. They commiserated with villagers who had been pillaged by ARVN troops and blamed the Vietnamese government and its American advisers for all the damages the tribesmen suffered in military actions. The Viet Cong offered the montagnards rudimentary medical services and, instead of taking from the montagnards, purchased animals and held feasts for the villagers. Through dialogue and example, they tried to demonstrate to the montagnards that the Viet Cong were their real friends. They made a big issue of the government's lack of respect for the montagnards, whom they addressed as sisters and brothers, and the government's despised assimilation policy. The Viet Cong were able to claim that they hadn't seized any tribal land or thrown any tribal leaders into jail. They played on the montagnards' desire for autonomy, promising that as soon as the South was liberated—with the help of the montagnards—they would give the montagnards autonomy, just as the North Vietnamese government had created autonomous tribal regions for the montagnards in the North. Ami Yoh never believed what she was told by the Viet Cong. "At first, the Viet Cong seemed better than the government," she says. "It wasn't surprising that many Rhade were won over by them. I didn't believe their sweet talk simply because they were Vietnamese, just as the government people were, and I wouldn't put much faith in anything any Vietnamese said."

Many montagnards became dedicated Viet Cong and still remain loyal to the Communist cause, but in general montagnard affection for the Viet Cong was short lived. The first VC cadres to work with the montagnards were hand-picked and expertly trained; later and more numerous cadres were neither as well behaved nor as able. "A few forgot what we really wanted was autonomy and started to talk about reunifying the country," Ami Yoh says. "We weren't the slightest bit interested in their slogan 'One nation under Hanoi.'" The Viet Cong found that propaganda alone was as ineffective in the mountains as it was in the lowlands and often supplemented their lectures with terrorism, especially when rebuffed by a particular village. The montagnards reacted to the terrorism earlier and more strongly than the Vietnamese in the lowlands, because they were victims of outsiders rather than of their own people. Sometimes, when the VC couldn't subvert a village, they would come into it and wait until they spotted planes flying overhead or some ARVN troops on an operation nearby. They would shoot at the planes or the troops, and then flee. The village was then often the object of an airstrike or an ARVN attack. As their infiltration through the highlands picked up and their need for supplies and labor increased, the Viet Cong no longer asked for food—they simply took rice from

95

the montagnards; instead of winning young montagnard boys over to their side through persuasion, they forcibly drafted them as soldiers, guides, and coolies. "Some Rhade who had been talked into joining the Viet Cong later wanted to leave them, but they were trapped," Ami Yoh says. "The Viet Cong would fire them up with rice wine and rage and get them to attack a village that had cooperated with the government. Once they returned to their senses and realized what they had done, they wanted to quit the Viet Cong. They couldn't, because the villagers would have punished them severely for the atrocities they had committed."

Just as Rhade disillusionment with the Viet Cong was mounting, the United States intervened directly into the developing struggle for the highlands and for a time gave the tribesmen new hope for improving their lot. In the late fall of 1961, the U. S. Central Intelligence Agency began a pilot counter-guerrilla project in the Rhade village of Buon Ea Nao, a few miles south of Ban Me Thuot. The villagers were offered arms to defend themselves against the Viet Cong and were promised material aid. An initial group of fifty men from the village were armed and given rudimentary military training by a U. S. Army Special Forces team on loan to the C.I.A. The group proved effective in defending its village and it was decided to make a similar offer to neighboring villages. The Rhade responded enthusiastically and flocked by the hundreds to Buon Ea Nao, which was transformed into a headquarters and training camp. The tribesmen saw the project as an opportunity to defend themselves against all Vietnamese, both government and Communist. The Rhade also tended to trust the Americans, because their relatively beneficial experience with the French made white men seem preferable to Vietnamese. They regarded the Americans as new protectors to replace the departed colonial administrators. Gradually, a complex of forty villages around Buon Ea Nao, most of which had been under Communist control, was pacified. Other complexes were grouped around secondary headquarters until two hundred villages in Darlac province had been secured. About fifteen thousand Rhade were armed and organized as village defenders, mobile strike companies to reinforce a village under attack, and surveillance teams and commandos to assess and interdict Viet Cong infiltration across the border from neighboring Cambodia. In order to eliminate friction with local Vietnamese officials, the Americans persuaded the Diem régime to remove the villages in the complex from the authority of the province and district chiefs and place them directly under a few carefully selected Vietnamese officers working with the Americans. The C.I.A. hoped to repeat the scheme with other tribes in the highlands and in this fashion to slowly pacify this strategic region. An opportunity for the government to make inroads among other tribes occurred in 1962. About one hundred thousand tribesmen fled their native villages that year because of Viet Cong oppression or because they were rounded up and brought into government-held areas by South Vietnamese troops. They were organized into strategic hamlets and promised help.

The very success of the Buon Ea Nao project, however, led to its demise. It aroused the deepest misgivings of President Ngo Dinh Diem and his powerful brother and political counselor, Ngo Dinh Nhu. They feared, as many other

senior Vietnamese officials did, and still do, that the United
States might encourage montagnard agitation for autonomy
and create a separate state in the highlands. In early 1963,
the South Vietnamese government put the villages in the
Buon Ea Nao and other complexes under the control of the
Vietnamese province and district chiefs. Within a few
months, the usual arrogance, neglect, and maladministration of Vietnamese officials had undone all the work of the
previous year. The disillusioned tribesmen ceased resisting
Viet Cong penetration and the complex soon reverted to
Communist control. Since then, the bulk of American work
with the montagnards has been limited to the hiring of
tribesmen as mercenaries at U. S. Army Special Forces
camps. Political affairs, propaganda, and village administration have become entirely the prerogative of the Vietnamese. The system has produced thousands of mercenaries, but
it does not appeal deeply to the tribesmen and does not
produce the kind of political cohesiveness necessary to resist the Viet Cong. The Vietnamese again proved incapable
of winning the loyalty of the tribes or administering the
villages effectively. Vietnamese Special Forces teams, which
worked with the Americans, also caused discord in the
camps themselves. The tribesmen who had fled or been
brought to government-held areas in 1962 were neglected,
and the Viet Cong gradually took over the strategic hamlets
in which montagnards had been relocated. By February of
1964, when Y'Bham was made deputy province chief of
Darlac, tribal grievances had reached serious proportions.
Y'Bham was not allowed any real authority and in resentment turned to renewed agitation for montagnard autonomy. In August of 1964, one hundred representatives of

various tribes met for three days and presented a list of demands to the Saigon government. The demands, aimed at ending the second-class citizenship of the montagnards, included compensation for land seized for Land Development Centers, special educational opportunities for montagnards (in order to narrow the cultural gap between the tribesmen and the Vietnamese), the right for montagnards to legally own land, primary schools for the tribesmen in their own languages, and the creation of a special directorate for montagnard affairs at cabinet level. The demands went unheeded and in September, hundreds of Rhade mercenaries in Special Forces camps in Darlac and the adjacent province of Quang Duc revolted and marched on Ban Me Thuot, seizing the radio station. The revolt was instigated by Y'Bham and staged in the name of a new inter-tribal autonomy organization he had secretly formed, called the United Front for the Struggle of the Oppressed Race. The Front is commonly known as Fulro, from the first letters of the French words for the same title. The rebels killed about thirty Vietnamese officers and soldiers at the camps and held a number of others hostage while they negotiated with Lieutenant General Nguyen Khanh, at that time the country's prime minister. Now, in addition to previous demands and several new ones, Fulro called upon the Saigon government to grant the tribes autonomous status within the Republic of South Viet Nam. Several U. S. Army officers and two American generals served as intermediaries during the negotiations. They finally persuaded the rebels to return to the camps and to release the Vietnamese hostages, which prevented further bloodshed. General Khanh promised to meet all the Fulro demands except that for autonomy, which he rejected. The revolt ended in a week. The camps involved were disbanded, the rebels were dispersed among other units, and Y'Bham and the principal Fulro leaders fled to refuge in Cambodia to await the implementation of General Khanh's promises. As in previous instances, however, the Saigon government made a few token gestures but no genuine effort to satisfy the tribesmen. Y'Bham remained in hiding in or near Cambodia and continued his agitation for autonomy. The Fulro movement spread among the tribes, particularly the mercenaries in the Special Forces camps, and Y'Bham organized his own armed bands. After dropping out of school, Y'Yoh disappeared. Ami Yoh has not seen him for many months, but she knows he is a member of Fulro and that he is off in the jungles with Y'Bham.

In 1965, Fulro continued to present its demands and the Vietnamese government continued to do its best to ignore them. In July, several hundred Rhade mercenaries at a U. S. Army Special Forces camp near Ban Me Thuot staged a non-violent mutiny; in September the Vietnamese forestalled a revolt by dissolving the camp and rounding up a nearby armed band of three hundred and fifty Fulro members. This firmness had only a transitory effect. In December, 1965, an armed montagnard revolt broke out. It was poorly organized, but thirty-four Vietnamese were killed before it was suppressed. A number of Fulro agents and sympathizers were arrested and four of the revolt's participants were sentenced to death. Repressive measures do not appear to be halting the growth of the Fulro movement. If anything, the disaffection with the Saigon government, particularly among the minority of educated and politically conscious tribesmen, seems to be increasing. New uprisings could occur at any time. Some American officials with experience in the highlands, realizing that the loyalty and support of the tribesmen is a prerequisite to the pacification of the region, would like to see the United States intervene vigorously to settle the unrest. So far, both Washington and the U. S. Embassy in Saigon have displayed a decided reluctance to do so. The maintenance of good relations with the Vietnamese military junta has taken priority and the montagnard problem remains unsolved. The Communists are making excellent use of their network of agents in the tribal villages. North Vietnamese prisoners captured in the fighting in the South speak of being guided along jungle trails by montagnards and of observing montagnard porters carrying supplies across the borders from Laos and Cambodia. Yet, as far as can be determined, the majority of the tribesmen favor neither Vietnamese side. They suffer the rule of whichever side happens to have troops or agents in their village at the moment. Most of the time, it is the Communists who are dominant. Above all, the tribesmen simply endure as best they can the agony of the war that has become a part of daily life in the highlands. Although Y'Bham and his supporters are not very effective now and the majority of Rhade not under Viet Cong control are neutral, rather than on the side of the Vietnamese government and the Americans, Ami Yoh, who is very sympathetic to Fulro, believes the organization could be a useful ally of the United States if the Americans made the Vietnamese redress some of the montagnard grievances. "As things stand now, this is not our war," she says. "If the Americans gave Fulro half the support they give the Vietnamese, the montagnards could clean out the highlands. Many Rhade have lost faith in the Americans, but I still place my hopes in them. They could help us if they wanted to. I don't understand why they don't want to. If the Americans don't look out for our interests, things will be terrible for the montagnards, no matter which side wins."

>>>>> *VI* <<<<<

>>>>> *L*e *Quang* is a thirteen-year-old orphan. He earns his living selling ice cream on the streets of Da Nang. He was born about forty miles from Da Nang, in Hoai Chau hamlet, Tuong An village, Quang Nam province, in the central lowlands of South Viet Nam. Quang's parents grew rice on a little over an acre of rented land until 1961, when his father enlisted in the Army. Quang, the oldest of six children, attended primary school in his native hamlet, studying Vietnamese, French, mathematics, and history. Although Quang has heard of Saigon, he has no idea where it is. He has never met any French people, and he wonders why he studied French. School was in session three and a half days a week; when Quang wasn't in school, he helped in the rice fields and took care of the family's two oxen. His help was especially needed after his father went into the Army and was stationed in another province.

Quang remembers dimly that there was peace in his area until he was seven. There has been fighting in and around Hoai Chau ever since. In 1963, Hoai Chau came under increasing Viet Cong dominance, and the Viet Cong instructed all the women in the hamlet whose husbands were in the government Army to talk them into deserting and returning home. Quang doesn't know whether his mother tried to persuade his father to desert. He knows only that his father stayed in the Army and that one evening while his mother was out fishing with some friends the Viet Cong stopped the sampan she was in, ordered her to disembark, and took her away. Her body was found a while later; she had been shot in the head. Quang's father learned about her death, but he couldn't come home. A few months later, he was killed in action. His body was brought back to Hoai Chau and was buried in the hamlet graveyard, not far from his wife's. The Viet Cong killed a number of men in Hoai Chau, but Quang's mother was the only woman they killed. The wives of other government soldiers were forced to go to a nearby Viet Cong mountain redoubt to attend political lectures, and then were released.

After their mother's death, Quang and his brothers and sisters remained in their parents' house. Relatives and neighbors helped care for them. Quang did many chores in return for the food they were given, but he was able to continue his schooling. In November, 1964, shortly after his father's death, floods struck the central lowlands. Many people drowned, thousands of buildings were swept away, crops were destroyed, and scores of animals, including Quang's oxen, perished. The grownups in Hoai Chau considered it too dangerous for the children to live alone any longer. Each of the six went to live with a different family of neighbors or relatives. One day, the waters rose to an alarming height; the neighbors Quang was staying with, their two small sons, five of their relatives, and Quang quickly boarded a sampan and paddled to Da Nang, the second-largest city in South Viet Nam. Everyone in the sampan was Catholic. In the late nineteen-fifties, the hamlet chief of Hoai Chau was a fanatical Catholic. He treated Catholics well and behaved badly toward non-Catholics. Most of the people in the hamlet changed their religion as a matter of self-interest. Hoai Chau benefited from the conversions, for Catholic hamlets received much more material aid from the Diem government than non-Catholic hamlets. Quang's parents, who had been Buddhists, became Catholics, partly because of the hamlet chief and partly because a relative who had joined the Army under Diem had discovered that Catholics were promoted much faster than non-Catholics, and urged their conversion.

It took the sampan containing Quang and the nine other people from Hoai Chau two days to reach Da Nang. Upon arriving in that busy port, they went to An Hai, one of many camps for flood victims that had been set up across the river from the main part of the city. An Hai had been organized by Catholics, and a priest from the hamlet had advised them to go there. During their first weeks at the An Hai camp, they slept in tents; later they were given a few sheets of steel and some money with which to build a hut. Quang went to work collecting firewood in the mountains around Da Nang. The men found employment as porters and laborers on the docks, and the women became fruit-and-vegetable vendors in the city's markets. Quang earned about forty piasters a day collecting firewood. He found the work strenuous and dull. In three months, he had saved two thousand piasters, and he took the money to an ice-cream company in the center of Da Nang, where he applied for a concession as an

ice-cream vendor. The company, which has many boys his
age among its concessionaires, requires a deposit of two
thousand piasters from every boy to whom it entrusts an
ice-cream box and a supply of ice cream. The money is re-
funded when the boy retires from the ice-cream trade. Quang
has now been selling popsicles for over a year.

When the weather is good, Quang shows up at the ice-
cream company early in the morning and fills his box—an
insulated wooden box with a metal top and a strap, which
he slings over his left shoulder. The box is painted bright
green; the name of the ice-cream company, the Vietnamese
words for "ice cream," and the likeness of a cow have been
splashed on in white. Packed with seventy small popsicles—
all it can hold—the box weighs over twenty-five pounds.
The company makes chocolate, orange, pineapple, and
vanilla popsicles. Chocolate sells best, and vanilla is least
popular. Quang has no jurisdiction over the variety he is
given to sell. Flavors are dispensed at the whim of the company manager. The popsicles sell for two piasters apiece.
Quang can refill his box at any time of the day or evening—
the company closes late and hardly ever runs out of popsicles
—and on a sunny day he can sell two to three hundred. He
earns three piasters for every ten popsicles he sells; his income averages seventy piasters per working day.

If the weather in Da Nang were nice every day of the
year, Quang would be quite affluent, for his daily expenses
average less than thirty piasters, but Da Nang has a rainy
season that lasts several months. Since few people buy ice
cream when the weather is bad, Quang doesn't go to the ice-
cream company on wet mornings. Some rainy days, he tries
to earn a few piasters by helping people tote produce from

one market to another. Carrying things is tiring and not very remunerative, so on other rainy days he doesn't bother to go to a market but instead visits the barracks of some of the thousands of American Marines stationed in and around Da Nang to see what he can salvage from their trash pails. Quang rather likes the American military, who buy ice cream from him when he is working, and occasionally grab his ice-cream box and try to help him sell his wares. When he visits the barracks, the Marines often kid around with him. "The American soldiers are funny and friendly people," Quang says. "They are very tall and husky, and they sometimes behave like children. They are cheerful, and they don't try to chase us off, the way Vietnamese soldiers do. Vietnamese soldiers don't like children hanging around. I don't know why." Some of the Marines whom Quang has met speak a little Vietnamese, and they have taught him a few words of English. He can count in English from one to ten and from fifteen to twenty; for some reason, his American acquaintances have not taught him the numbers eleven through fourteen. Quang doesn't know the names of any famous Americans—past or present Presidents, or ambassadors to South Viet Nam. The only Americans he knows by name are two Marines, Tom and Bill. Quang finds the GIs generous with cigarettes and candy. He eats the candy with pleasure; since he doesn't smoke, he passes the cigarettes on to contemporaries who do. The English vocabulary of most urchins in Da Nang includes the words "Give me one dollar." Quang has never asked for money. "I think I can always earn enough so that I can eat," he says. "So far I've always had a few piasters in my pocket." Quang and his friends appreciate the access they are usually accorded to the American soldiers' trash pails. "When the garbage is old, the GIs try to prevent us from picking things up, because we usually eat and drink whatever is left in the cans and bottles they throw out," he says. "They always say it's not good for us, and we have to play many tricks on them to get at it. But if the garbage is fresh, they let us collect whatever we want."

Almost all of Quang's clothes derive from GI trash cans. He has two olive-drab shirts and two pairs of olive-drab trousers. A tailor in Da Nang cut his two outfits down to size for him from two discarded Marine uniforms for forty-five piasters apiece. The rest of his wardrobe consists of one pair of rubber sandals, which he bought for twenty-five piasters, and one old Marine fatigue cap. Quang is a dark-skinned boy with coarse features, and he looks about ten years old. He cuts a dignified olive-drab figure as he walks along, manfully carrying his heavy working equipment and pushing the peak of his oversize cap up from his eyes. Life on the streets, where he often sleeps as well as works, has not improved the quality of his Vietnamese—he slurs many of his words—but it has not yet impaired his honesty or his pleasant disposition.

Quang doesn't cross the river from the main part of Da Nang to the An Hai camp every night, although he can commute free. The usual boat fare is one piaster. One-piaster coins, which the boatmen need in order to make change for five- and ten-piaster bills handed them by passengers, are always in short supply. Quang is generally paid for his ice cream in small change. For ten one-piaster coins the boatmen give him a ten-piaster bill and a free ride across the river; this arrangement suits Quang, since he doesn't like to spend one unnecessary piaster. The last sampans and ferries leave for An Hai around eight o'clock at night, however, and if Quang crosses the river at that time he loses his chance to sell ice cream to evening strollers and movie-goers. "It's in the evening that you can often make the most money," he says. On clear nights, Quang prefers to work late and sleep in the city—sometimes in a movie theater or under a movie marquee.

When Quang does return to An Hai for the night, he doesn't have a home, or even a bed, to return to. The nine people with whom he left Hoai Chau were able to build only a tiny hut, which is divided into two rooms and furnished with just three bamboo beds. In one room, four men and two young boys sleep on two of the beds; in the other room three women sleep on the third bed. Since there is no place in the hut for Quang when he comes to An Hai, he sleeps on the concrete floor of the camp church, along with many other homeless people. He hasn't invested in any such luxury as a sleeping mat, a blanket, or a mosquito net; he does have some rice sacks to lie on (they are adorned with the United States Aid symbol of clasped hands) and he doesn't mind sleeping on the church floor. "There aren't many mosquitoes, it's very cool, I have other kids to talk to, and there's plenty of room there," he says. After spending a night in the church, he goes to the hut of his former sampan-mates for breakfast. "They give me some rice to eat in the morning and they don't take money for it, although they are quite poor," he says. "They treat me quite well. But I am not one of the family." Quang goes to An Hai at least once a week. He keeps his rice sacks and his spare outfit there—he has no other possessions—and he takes a weekly bath beside the camp well. He washes his clothes in the river every second or third night, wherever he has chosen to sleep.

During the dry season, Quang works a seven-day week. Sunday, an excellent day for selling ice cream, he gets up very early, sells one boxful of popsicles, attends Mass, and then goes to the company to refill his box. The rainy season prevents him from saving much money, because his expenses are the same all year round. He always spends five piasters for lunch and five for dinner; each meal is a bowl of rice with soy sauce, or a small portion of fish. He usually has tea with his meals and drinks a glass of cold water at the ice-cream company on his reloading expeditions. He buys his own breakfast, unless he is at An Hai, and he indulges in oc-casional snacks, including two of his own popsicles a day. Bimonthly haircuts cost him five piasters. From time to time, he has a headache, and then he goes to a drugstore to buy a few piasters worth of common headache pills. Quang had typhoid fever at the age of seven, and his family was afraid he would die; a practitioner of traditional medicine in his hamlet was credited with saving his life. He has had no serious illness since his arrival in Da Nang, and he knows nothing about the medical facilities there. Quang has not had to buy clothes for a long time; the cloth of his two outfits is very sturdy, and the tailor altered them with room for him to grow in. He buys his meals at the same place every day, a sidewalk stand run by a woman, al-though the food at her stand is no better or cheaper than the food sold elsewhere in Da Nang and the woman shows no signs of appreciating his regular patronage. "She's all right, but she's not particularly friendly," Quang says. "She doesn't talk to me. I don't have conversations with grown-

ups. I buy food from her just because I know her stand."
Quang is friendly with several of his ice-cream-selling col-
leagues, and talks with them every day; he has no best friend.
He has never been harassed by the police. "The cops only
chase boys who hang around outside GI bars and beg," he
says. "They don't bother me, because I'm selling ice cream
honestly." No one has ever tried to put Quang in an orphan-
age, and he is glad. He has no clear idea of what an orphan-
age is like, but he knows without ever having seen one
that he prefers his freedom, even though it exposes him to
certain perils, such as older boys who bully him from time
to time. "They want to take ice cream without paying for
it, and they threaten to beat me up," he says. "They haven't
been able to so far. I've always managed to run away."

When Quang left Hoai Chau on the sampan, he expected to be reunited with his brothers and sisters in his
hamlet as soon as the floodwaters subsided, but shortly
after he reached Da Nang, Viet Cong strength increased in
his region. He has heard that the Viet Cong attacked his
hamlet and wiped out the militia, and that some of the
people of the hamlet were killed in the crossfire, although
they had all been told to build underground shelters in
which to take refuge when shooting started. The hamlet was
then bombed several times. "I know of five whole families
who were wiped out by the bombs," he says. "Leaflets were
dropped five days before the bombing, warning them to go
away from the hamlet, but they didn't, or maybe they
couldn't." Quang has been told that American troops staged
an operation in his region not long ago. They arrived in helicopters and occupied Hoai Chau for a while. As soon as they
went away, the Viet Cong returned. It would be imprudent

for Quang to go back to his hamlet now, because the Viet Cong control it and are drafting boys his age. "I guess some of my neighbors were with the Viet Cong before," Quang says. "Now I think all of them have to be on the Viet Cong side. I don't think they are active fighting men. They just have to cooperate with Viet Cong units." Quang isn't sure where his brothers and sisters are living. Some of them may still be in the vicinity of Hoai Chau; others may have been taken to barracks some miles away by several of his uncles who are soldiers.

Quang doesn't weep when he talks about the loss of his parents. He weeps only when he talks about school. He seems to associate education with the happier life he had in the past in Hoai Chau and with the possibility of leading a decent life in the future. "In my hamlet, I was able to go to school even after my father's death," he says. "I was in the fifth year of primary school—the last year—when the floods came and washed everything away. If there were peace back home, I could go to secondary school and work in the fields as well. School is quite cheap at home, and you don't need much money there for other things, either. We always got enough to eat. We could find fish, crabs, and all kinds of different vegetables in the river. I had to stop my education only after I left my father's hamlet." If Quang went to school in Da Nang, he wouldn't have time to earn enough money to live on, let alone cover his school expenses. He doesn't know what he would like to be when he grows up, but he doesn't want to sell ice cream indefinitely. "A good education is necessary if you want to be a priest or a teacher," he says. "Also, the better your education, the better the life you have in the Army."

If an American soldier offered to adopt Quang, take him to the United States, and give him a good education, he wouldn't accept. "I only want to return to my hamlet, even though I don't really expect to," he says. "I don't know how the war started, and I can't believe it will ever end. I would like to see my brothers and sisters soon, because I'm afraid that if I don't we'll no longer be able to recognize each other. I was quite happy in Hoai Chau, even after my parents died. I worked hard, but I enjoyed the company of my brothers and sisters and our neighbors and relatives. I was able to go to school. I didn't have to worry about the future. Here in Da Nang, I'm too busy in the daytime to feel sorry for myself. Sometimes I cry at night, after I've said my prayers and before I fall asleep—when I realize that I don't mean anything to anyone and that I'm alone in the world."

>>>>> *VII* <<<<<

>>>>> *Bui Tuan,* or Hanh Duc as he has been called in recent years, is a Buddhist monk. He was born twenty years ago in a village in Quang Tri, now the northern-most province of South Viet Nam. Hanh Duc, whose parents are poor rice farmers, was the oldest of seven children. As a boy he alternately went to school and did light work in the rice fields (depending on the state of the family's finances), helped care for his younger sister and five younger brothers, and spent a good deal of his time in the pagoda in his hamlet. When he was thirteen, he decided he wanted to become a monk. His parents were reluctant to give their consent—they were not particularly devout Buddhists and they wanted their oldest son to choose a line of work that would enable him to remain at home. Before Hanh Duc could persuade his mother and father to give their permission, two of his brothers died suddenly of illness. "I couldn't leave my parents with their sorrow so I had to stay home for three more years," he says. "But after the death of my brothers, I finally succeeded in making my parents understand the futility of life. In the local pagoda the monks had

convinced me that existence was suffering, that our passions are the origin of our suffering, and that if I became a monk I would learn to do away with my passions. I decided it would be best for me to spend my life in the shade of the Buddha." Hanh Duc is a humorless young man with a sallow complexion and long nails on his little fingers—the traditional affectation of a Vietnamese man who does not work with his hands. His shaved head and sparse eyebrows help give him a rather blank expression.

It is estimated that seventy to eighty per cent of South Viet Nam's approximately sixteen million inhabitants consider themselves Buddhists. Only about half this number, however, regularly frequent pagodas. The others practice a mixture of Buddhism, Taoism, Confucianism, and animism, and worship at ancestral altars in their homes. Two branches of Buddhism are prevalent in the country—the Lesser Vehicle (Theravada or Hinayana) and the Greater Vehicle (Mahayana). The Hinayana branch is found mainly in the southern and western parts of South Viet Nam. These areas were formerly portions of the ancient Cambodian empire, to which Buddhism spread directly from India. Hinayana is the more conservative of the two branches. Its saffron-robed monks walk barefooted, begging for their food, adhere strictly to Buddhist traditions (such as not eating after noon), and do not concern themselves with worldly matters. The Mahayana branch, which originally spread into what is now North Viet Nam from China, where Buddhism had undergone a transformation, is dominant in central Viet Nam. It is more progressive than Hinayana. In recent years, the leading Mahayana monks have been very much involved with such worldly matters as politics. Their interpretation

of the traditional Buddhist vows of poverty does not pre-
clude stereophonic record players, air conditioners, electric
razors, transistor radios, and chauffeur-driven Mercedes-
Benz sedans. Mahayana monks wear gray and brown robes
for everyday dress and yellow robes on ceremonial occasions.
They do not beg for their food, but instead solicit contributions in money or goods from the faithful at the pagodas or
by calling at the homes of regular donors.

The Mahayana monks first entered politics in May of
1963, when they lanuched a campaign to overthrow the
régime of President Ngo Dinh Diem, a Roman Catholic.
One of the weapons employed against the Diem régime was
suicide by fire. Buddhist monks, nuns, and faithful burned
themselves to death to protest the government's policies.
This effective campaign caught the imagination of the Vietnamese and transformed into active opposition the widespread but hitherto simmering unrest with the Diem government. The suicides also shocked international opinion and
forced the United States to disavow President Diem. The
result was the coup d'état by the South Vietnamese Army
in November, 1963, and the assassination of President Diem.
Since then, the Mahayana leaders have played a key role in
bringing down two other Saigon governments, and have
been a force for any Saigon régime to reckon with. A militant
faction of Mahayana monks, led by Venerable Tri Quang,
has consistently displayed neutralist political tendencies,
and an opposition to the war against the Viet Cong guerrillas and to the American presence in South Viet Nam.
Although the development of Buddhism in North Viet
Nam has been fettered by the Communist régime there,
these militant Buddhist leaders show little fear of being

unable to compete successfully with the Communists in the South. Hanh Duc is a Mahayana monk.

In early 1962, Hanh Duc applied to the provincial Buddhist representatives in Quang Tri; he was accepted as a novice monk and was assigned to a pagoda in a village a few miles from his home. Eight other monks lived at the pagoda—three older men and five boys about his age. The senior monk at the pagoda chose the Buddhist name of Hanh Duc for him, by which he was henceforth known. Hanh Duc's head was shaved, in accordance with Buddhist custom. For clothing, he was given ankle-length gray robes which fastened at the side. He was immediately obligated to obey the five cardinal Buddhist regulations—Do Not Kill, Do Not Steal, Do Not Have Sexual Relations with Women, Do Not Lie, and Do Not Drink Alcoholic Beverages. And he began to study the four basic Buddhist books of prayers, regulations, manners, and doctrine. These books are written in classical Chinese characters, which Hanh Duc had to memorize. He devoted seven hours a day to his Buddhist studies and prayers. The rest of his time was spent on household tasks and gardening. Life at the pagoda was uneventful until the Buddhist struggle against the Diem régime in 1963. "My pagoda wasn't raided by the police, but the government hired some people to throw stones at it," Hanh Duc says. "I was pretty active in the Buddhist campaign against Mr. Diem. I didn't volunteer to set myself on fire. I led schoolchildren in demonstrations and on visits to monks who were fasting in protest against Mr. Diem, because that's what the older monks told me to do. Mr. Diem's death didn't make me joyful, although I was glad to know that with the overthrow of his régime, a threat to Buddhism had been eliminated."

In early 1964, Hanh Duc passed his examinations on the first four books of Buddhism and advanced one rank to the second level in the Buddhist clerical hierarchy. He was given a new set of gray robes, which fastened down the front. He was now bound by five additional Buddhist regulations—Do Not Use Cosmetics, Do Not Attend Movies or the Theater, Do Not Sleep on a Comfortable Bed or a Large Mat, Do Not Eat outside of Prescribed Hours, and Do Not Possess Any Precious Things. He was transferred to Gia Lam pagoda in Hue, the former imperial capital of Viet Nam and a stronghold of Mahayana Buddhism. Hanh Duc may stay in Gia Lam pagoda in Hue for another ten or twenty years; he may be transferred to a pagoda somewhere else in the country at any time, at the discretion of his superiors. Gia Lam pagoda is a damp one-story concrete building faced with yellow stucco. It consists of a large shrine, where an imposing gilt statue of the Buddha is kept, a reception room, where visitors are served strong tea, and several dormitory-style bedrooms furnished with double-decker bunks. It is inhabited by eight young monks, three older monks, and two elderly widows, who do the cooking.

Many older Buddhist monks are unable to read and write Vietnamese; they did not attend lay schools and studied only Buddhist books in Chinese characters in their pagodas. Nowadays, virtually all young Mahayana monks are given a primary education and many continue their secondary studies at Buddhist or secular schools. A few attend univer-

123

sities in Viet Nam and abroad; one Mahayana leader did postgraduate work at Yale University. Of the eight young monks at Gia Lam pagoda, three are attending secondary school. Five, including Hanh Duc, who are not intellectually gifted, are simply continuing their Buddhist studies; while the others take up foreign languages, history, geography, and mathematics, they do social work at Buddhist-sponsored orphanages and dispensaries, visit the homes of the faithful to say prayers for sick members of the family or for the dead, and make the rounds of donors, who contribute money and material goods to the pagoda and its projects. "I could continue my academic studies if I insisted," Hanh Duc says. "I was in the first year of secondary school when I left my family. But I prefer social work and Buddhist studies, and am content to let the others go to school. There must be different people to do different jobs."

A monk is eligible to go from the second to the third notch in the clergy once he is twenty years old and has passed examinations on a dozen books of Buddhist studies. At the third level, he receives the title *Thich*, a religious honorific, and is technically obligated to follow two hundred and forty additional regulations. Some monks attain this rank soon after they are twenty, some never do. It takes a minimum of twenty years to go from the third to the fourth rank, whereupon a monk should follow fifty-eight more regulations. Only a handful of monks at any time are elevated to the fifth level. They are expected to follow still another fifty-eight regulations. No senior monk appears to know or to follow all of the numerous regulations on the higher levels. Their observance seems to depend largely on personal convenience or desire. A monk who does not smoke will cite a ban against smoking as one of the regulations; a chain smoker will not.

Hanh Duc rises every day at four o'clock in the morning. Two of the eight junior monks beat the pagoda's bell one hundred and eight times between four o'clock and five o'clock as an exhortation to prayer. The young monks take turns beating the bell—one month they are on bell duty every other morning, the following month every other evening from seven-thirty until eight-thirty. Those monks not on morning bell duty study their academic or religious lessons until five o'clock, when collective prayers are chanted for an hour. From six to seven o'clock in the morning, the young monks learn how to perform religious ceremonies. From seven till eleven-thirty, two of the young monks go to secondary schools, while Hanh Duc and the other non-academic monks do household chores and then set out on their social welfare missions. Hanh Duc gives shots to patients in Buddhist dispensaries and washes their clothes. In Buddhist orphanages, he helps bathe the children and tells them stories with Buddhist morals. At eleven-thirty, he returns to Gia Lam, where collective prayers are sung for half an hour. At noon, the monks eat lunch, the first of their two daily meals. Lunch and dinner consist of rice and vegetables, or rice with vegetable oil or soy sauce, and soybean cakes. The widows show considerable ingenuity with soybeans, serving them fried, boiled, or pickled. The final test of a cook's talent is to produce a soybean cake that can pass for a pork chop. The monks are vegetarians; they drink milk but eat no meat, fish, or eggs. "I stopped eating living creatures a month before I left my family and I haven't eaten any since," Hanh Duc says. "I don't think I could eat meat or fish now. I even resent the smell." He is oblivious to the aroma of boiled cabbage, which permeates the pagoda. Monks are not allowed to eat more than two meals, even on a feast day, and they are not permitted to eat between meals. Hanh Duc says the only exception to the eating-between-meals rule is for young boys who enter pagodas and become novices at the early ages of five to ten. Hanh Duc has heard of *Thich* Tri Quang, the leader of the militant Mahayana monks, but he has not seen him wolf down Hershey chocolate kisses throughout the day; many foreign journalists who have interviewed Tri Quang have.

After lunch, Hanh Duc takes a siesta or does as he pleases until two o'clock. From two to four-thirty, four days a week, he pursues his Buddhist studies; the other three days, he uses those hours to putter around the pagoda and its grounds doing housework and gardening. From four-thirty to six o'clock, Hanh Duc is again free. Dinner is at six, and is followed by collective prayers and bell-beating for two of the young monks. From eight-thirty to ten-thirty, Hanh Duc studies his Buddhist lessons, while some of his friends recite their French verbs and grapple with elementary algebra. Bedtime and lights out are at ten-thirty; only monks who are preparing for examinations may stay up past that hour. Hanh Duc doesn't especially like to beat the pagoda bell—the young monks occasionally quarrel about whose turn it is—but he accepts it as his duty. "We tease each other from time to time about the bell and about the length of our haircuts," he says. "We shave each other's heads about twice a month. We never go too far in our joking and we never kid around with the older monks. We lead a very austere and serious life." This staid life suits

Hanh Duc. It is also a secure existence. If Hanh Duc needs anything, such as medical care, he has only to ask one of the older monks and it is provided. "I've even been treated by a western-educated doctor," he says. He feels cheerful after he prays. He particularly enjoys doing charitable work and helping unhappy people. "I sometimes resent the faithful who ask us to pray for their dead and then press money on us as if we charged a fee for praying," he says. "There is a polite way for people to make donations to the pagoda if they wish to do so. I make a distinction between praying and soliciting funds."

Hanh Duc has enjoyed his first four years of Buddhist studies. He appears to have spent most of this time mastering the Chinese characters in which the books are written, because he does not yet seem to know a great deal about Buddhism. He has no idea when Gautama the Buddha is said to have lived, or what the Eightfold Path to Enlightenment is; he knows the five cardinal Buddhist regulations by heart, but has to look up the second five in a book. His principal theological accomplishment is explaining the flexibility of Mahayana Buddhism. "Even the five cardinal regulations need not be followed under certain circumstances," he says. "Buddhism is a religion of compassion. It is wrong to kill anyone or anything, because if you kill a living creature you inflict suffering on it. But if a tiger comes to a village and endangers the villagers' lives, it is all right to kill it, though when you do so you face bad consequences in your next reincarnation so you really must kill out of self-forgetfulness. It is even permissible to kill a man, if his death will be beneficial to a great number of people. Once, the Buddha was traveling in a boat with a hundred men who were partners in a successful business. The Buddha learned that one man intended to kill the other ninety-nine to get their share of the profits for himself. The Buddha decided to kill him to save the other ninety-nine." In similar fashion, the leading Mahayana monks have justified street violence and fiery suicides by claiming that the Buddhist faith had been endangered by any of a number of Saigon governments. They are chronically unable to cite precise scriptural authority for their actions. Hanh Duc, who owns a wristwatch, says that the regulation about monks' possessing valuables is also flexible. "We must adapt ourselves to existing conditions," he says. "We have to follow some kind of a schedule in civilized life, so a watch becomes necessary. I'm not entitled to own money, but I must sometimes carry it so that I can buy things to meet my personal needs, such as busfare when I travel home to see my family. I must never lose sight of the purpose of the watch and the money."

Hanh Duc is allowed to go home twice a year for two or three days, to visit his family. His hamlet is near a district town and is fairly secure. He makes the forty-mile journey home by bus. The road is usually safe, though sometimes a couple of bridges are out, having been blown up by Viet Cong mines or American bombs. "I pay visits to my family only to show my filial devotion," Hanh Duc says. "Even when I'm in my hamlet, I spend the nights and as much of my time there as possible in the local pagoda, where I feel more at home. Since I've left my parents, they have become more devout. They go without meat and fish twice a month now. I'm glad about that." Hanh Duc's sister and two of his brothers still live at home; his third brother lives in Hue, where he is studying to become a mechanic. Hanh Duc seldom sees him. "Everything is futile and unreal—even families," Hanh Duc says. "This watch on my wrist may not be there at all."

Hanh Duc becomes irascible when the subject of politics is broached. "We never have political discussions in the pagoda," he says. "We leave it to the senior monks to decide whether Buddhism is being discriminated against by the government in power. They frequently hold meetings to discuss such matters. I do whatever my superiors tell me to do. If they want me to demonstrate against the government, I go out to demonstrate. I'm not interested in worldly affairs so it's best for me to be told what's expected of me. Personally, I don't care who's in power. I consider power and riches futile and unreal."

Hanh Duc takes as little interest in the war as he does in his family or in politics. A few of his childhood friends are fighting with the Viet Cong; more of his old friends and relatives are on the government side, and some of them have been killed. "An uncle of mine was wounded in action," Hanh Duc says. "He's now in a hospital in Hue and since I go there anyway to do social work, I sometimes visit him. We say prayers for peace every day in the pagoda, but I don't follow the war in the newspapers. I don't like to read stories about the killing and fighting everywhere. I just feel sorry for the country, because it is being chewed up by the war, and I pray fervently for the war to be ended as soon as possible. I don't care who wins, because I have no idea which side will turn out to be good or bad for Buddhism. I just wish we'd be left alone to practice our religion."

>>>>> *VIII* <<<<<

>>>>>> *Private Pham Van Loc* has been a soldier in the Army of the Republic of Viet Nam for six of the last eight years. Loc was born sometime in 1937 in a village in Quang Nam province in the central lowlands of South Viet Nam (formerly the French protectorate of Annam). When he was thirteen, Loc started primary school and attended it for five years, first in his own hamlet, later in nearby hamlets where his parents sent him to live with relatives to avoid his being drafted by the French. He liked school (mathematics was his favorite subject, he hated dictation) and wanted to continue, but his parents, who worked in the rice fields for landlords, couldn't afford to keep him in school. Loc was the oldest living child in the family. Three of his older brothers and one older sister (as well as one younger brother) died of illness before they reached the age of five; a younger brother and a younger sister are still living. When he stopped going to school, he worked in the rice fields for two years. In 1955, the year Loc left school, he received his draft notice and in 1957 was actually drafted. One day in July, 1957, he and the other draftees from his

area were taken to a reception center in the nearby city of Da Nang, where they spent one week doing nothing but filling out forms, receiving boots and uniforms, and bemoaning the fact that they weren't allowed out to see the city. After a week, the draftees were flown to the Quang Trung Army training center, near Saigon. They spent their first month there clearing wasteland for new barracks and their next four months receiving military training. They learned a little judo, they were shown how to fire an array of weapons, and they were taught to march, run, and crawl. They received no political training. The food wasn't good at Quang Trung, but the draftees objected less to the food than to the fact that they were granted only a fleeting glimpse of Saigon before leaving the training center. After five months at Quang Trung, Loc was sent to an Army camp in the delta for three months, and then to one on the central coast for three months. "I never fired a shot at anyone during my first year in the Army," Loc says. "All I did was clear land, paint walls, and train too hard on too little food. I found life miserable from the first day, and wished to finish my twelve-month term. I knew I was trained to fight the new Viet Minh, but I was never much interested in fighting them. The old Viet Minh had fought the French, and I hadn't liked the French very much. They cut down all the trees in our garden for what they said were security reasons. I wasn't for or against either side in those days—I only wanted the fighting to stop. I didn't know anything about the new Viet Minh. I was just drafted and I tried to fulfill my obligation."

Loc was released in June, 1958, and he returned to his hamlet and resumed work in the rice fields. His parents arranged a marriage for him to a girl a year older than he from a nearby village. Although his marriage has been only "so-so," Loc thinks it is good for parents to choose wives for their sons. "If we did our own choosing, we might make more serious mistakes or choose wives who would displease our parents," he says. Loc's hamlet was serene in the late fifties and he was unaware that the Viet Cong had become very active elsewhere until October, 1960, when he was called back to the Army, not as a draftee but as a regular, for an indefinite stay. He was given one month of military training at Da Nang; he received no political training. He was then assigned to the Second Infantry Division, stationed in Da Nang. After five months, he was transferred to the Seventh Infantry Division, stationed in the delta. "The government was afraid I wouldn't fight well if I stayed too close to my home," Loc says. "I was sorry to be transferred." Loc has been stationed in various provinces in the delta over the last five years. He is currently a member of a heavy weapons squad, in a company of an infantry battalion, based at My Tho, the capital of Dinh Tuong province, fifty miles southwest of Saigon.

Loc, a shy, quiet twenty-nine-year-old of medium build, who seems very resigned to his lot in life, has gone out on hundreds of patrols, ambushes, and operations since 1961. He came under fire for the first time one day in February, 1962, when his battalion went to search for some Viet Cong who had harassed an outpost the previous night. The men were wading through some rice paddies when they drew fire from a village they were approaching. As they fought their way into the village, six soldiers were killed by the Viet Cong. By the time they got into the village, the VC had fled. They found three VC bodies and were told by the villagers that the Viet Cong had carried away a number of dead and wounded. The biggest battle in which Loc has been involved was a similar operation, in July, 1963, when his battalion attacked a village that was flying a VC flag. It took his company an hour and a half to fight its way into the village across a rice paddy. They had heavy air support. The VC eventually fled. Loc's battalion lost about eighteen soldiers and counted fifty-eight VC bodies. Many of the Viet Cong were killed by bombs dropped from the planes and by the machine guns of the armored personnel carriers supporting them. "We would have a much harder time if the VC had airplanes," Loc says.

Loc has been wounded in action once. Late in the afternoon of December 27, 1964, as his battalion was entering a hamlet to search for Viet Cong, the men drew fire. A heavy engagement ensued. By seven o'clock, the battalion had been badly mauled and was withdrawing, when Loc was hit in the forearm. It was getting dark and he couldn't see much, but knowing the Viet Cong were in the hamlet, he ran in the opposite direction. After a while, he met up with a fleeing friend, gave him his gun, and told him he had been hit and that he was going to hide in the jungle for the night. The jungle was thick and Loc wasn't afraid the Viet Cong would find him. The wound was painful but bearable. The VC withdrew before daylight. Loc's battalion came back the next morning and picked him up. He was given first aid, taken by helicopter to regimental headquarters in Ben Tre, the capital of the delta province of Kien Hoa, and then to a hospital in My Tho, where his arm was X-rayed and put in a cast. He spent four weeks in the hospital. He is not sure if he was hit by a bullet or by a piece of shrapnel, but whatever hit his arm lodged in the radius and is still there, because the doctors said the bone would be broken if they removed anything. When the weather is sultry, the arm still hurts.

Loc spends much more of his time in the Army waiting to fight than fighting. A recent ten-day period was typical for him. On Friday, his company went by truck from My Tho to Sung Hieu, another district in Dinh Tuong province, to stand by while the Sung Hieu troops were out on an operation. They stayed there until Monday. On Tuesday, they returned to My Tho; Loc's company was on standby while the other companies of his battalion were out on an operation. On Wednesday, at six in the morning, Loc's company was ordered to Long Dinh, another district in Dinh Tuong province. They went by truck to the district capital and then walked across flooded rice paddies for several miles, stopping at noon for lunch and a siesta. At four in the afternoon, they approached what the soldiers were told was a VC grenade factory. As they drew near, the Viet Cong sniped at them, and Loc's company fired back. The company sustained no casualties; Loc doesn't think they wounded or killed any VC. His company took the factory after the Viet Cong had fled. They seized about six hundred grenades and three or four hundred mines and burned down the factory huts. They walked back to the Long Dinh district town, and returned to My Tho by truck. "We didn't know the object of the operation when we set out," Loc says. "We just found ourselves approaching the factory at four o'clock and when the VC fired at us, we fired at them. Soldiers aren't entitled to know in advance where they are going. That's for officers to know." On Thursday

137

and Friday, Loc's company rested and was on standby in My Tho. On Saturday morning, Loc got permission to go into town. He was there when his company received an order at one o'clock in the afternoon to go out immediately; he missed the operation and spent an idle day, except for the two hours extra guard duty he was given that night, along with a scolding—"a matter of formality," he says. When his friends returned at eight o'clock Saturday evening, they said they had been to Cho Gao, a district in Dinh Tuong. They had walked through some rice paddies and had had no contact with the VC. "That's the way the majority of operations go," Loc says. "No success, no failure, no contact with the Viet Cong." On Sunday, his company was again on standby in My Tho. Sometimes, Loc sleeps in barracks; sometimes, when he goes out on an operation of several days duration, he sleeps in the jungle. His company is currently encamped in a residential section of My Tho. "We've been told to ask the people if they're agreeable to our spending the night in their houses," he says. "Most of them are, but if there aren't enough beds to go around, some of us have to spend the night outdoors. I prefer to sleep in a hammock outside, because I like fresh air and I feel free. In a house, I'm very likely to be bothered by children."

On most of the recent operations Loc has been a crewman on a sixty millimeter mortar, but occasionally he carries a rifle or a submachine gun instead. "I like firing very much, and sometimes when I'm assigned a small weapon, I fire a few shots at nothing in particular," he says. "We always have enough ammunition. I've seen many Viet Cong killed in the actions I've taken part in and I've done a lot of firing, but I'm not sure if I've actually killed any VC. It's hard to tell whose gun has done what." Loc has never captured a VC or talked to one. He doesn't consider himself qualified to judge the Viet Cong's fighting ability because he hasn't fought in enough big battles against them, but from the operations he has taken part in he admires their cleverness at escaping. "The VC aren't as well armed and equipped as we are, and they endure more hardships, and perhaps that's why they're more resourceful than we are most of the time," he says. "We go out to hunt for them and we can't find them and suddenly they attack us from behind. They must be very crafty people. They have a knack for appearing from nowhere, shooting at us, and then disappearing again. We do well against them when we're well led, but often our officers don't seem eager to find the VC or to fight them when we've got them pretty well cornered; they let them escape instead. Still, it's not my place to criticize officers. Criticism of officers isn't forbidden, but I don't think I have any right to do that. Once in a great while, officers chew us out for not following their orders on an operation, but they don't criticize or discipline us much."

Loc has not been able to return to his native hamlet since he was transferred to the delta in 1961. It is practically impossible for soldiers to get a long leave—two weeks off. Loc hasn't had one long leave since he entered the Army and he can't make a round-trip to the central lowlands when he gets short leave—five days. He exchanged letters with his parents from 1961 until mid-1964. In the last two years, he has continued to write to his parents every couple of months. He has received no reply. He doesn't know why, because his hamlet used to be pretty secure. He wonders if the Viet Cong have taken over the hamlet, or if his parents have moved away, or if they have died. He wishes he could go home to find out. Loc might have lost touch with his wife, too, if she had stayed at home, but she decided to follow him south soon after he was transferred to the delta. She now lives near regimental headquarters in Ben Tre, about ten miles from My Tho. Every three or four months, Loc gets five days off and visits her, and his wife comes to see him every few weeks. When she comes to see him, she brings their two daughters, a three-year-old and a five-year-old. She comes early in the morning and leaves in the afternoon. Loc has forbidden her to come in recent weeks because she is pregnant. He is already looking forward to the seven days leave he will be entitled to when his third child is born in a few months.

Loc receives a total of 3,538 piasters a month—1,558 piasters basic pay, plus 555 piasters for food provided by his unit, plus 1,425 piasters family allowance, which will increase when his third child is born. He thinks American soldiers are paid about three times as much as he is, and he knows that the VC are paid nothing at all. Loc has to buy his own breakfast—the 555 piasters for food covers only lunch and dinner, usually rice and fish, vegetables, and *nuoc mam*. "When food used to be less expensive, we got pretty good food," Loc says. "Nowadays, it's a little bit hard, but I think the food is good enough. I don't feel the need to eat in restaurants." Instead of sending only his 1,425 piasters family allowance to his wife, Loc sends her 2,000 piasters and worries about even that not being enough. Her expenses in Ben Tre are higher than they would be at home, and their income is lower. In their own hamlet, he and his wife would both work in the rice fields; relatives would help care for the children. They would build their own home and pay no rent. In Ben Tre, Loc's wife has to rent a house, and since it is a city she cannot find work, because the only work she knows is rice growing. At home, Loc and his family would have better clothes and medical care, and they could save five hundred to a thousand piasters a month "for a rainy day and to buy some land." After paying for his lunches and dinners and sending money to his wife, Loc has only 983 piasters a month left for himself, which he spends on haircuts, cigarettes, breakfasts, soft drinks, an occasional rice brandy "to cheer myself up," an infrequent movie, and two lottery tickets a week. He dreams of winning first prize in the national lottery and having enough money to live in Saigon and to enjoy life as he imagines people there do. "I never spend a piaster for a bad girl," Loc says. "And I never save a piaster." In the six years that Loc has been a regular in the Army, he has received only one raise, of 113 piasters a month, a year ago. He is soon due for a second raise, of about 200 piasters a month. A private's pay is low, and however long he stays in the Army, Loc expects to remain a private. "If you fight well, you may get decorated, but your chances of getting promoted are pretty slim," Loc says. "To get promoted, you have to have had a good formal education."

Loc has heard that there are Viet Cong infiltrators in the Army, but he doesn't think there are any in his company. He and many of the men in his company, who are from all over South Viet Nam, are close friends. Loc thinks the best thing about the Army is that he will have friends throughout the country when the war is over. Loc knows

141

the full name of his company commander and the first name and rank of his battalion commander, but not his family name; he doesn't know the names of the commander of his regiment and division. He knows how the war is going in his section of the delta; he doesn't hear of its progress elsewhere in the country. Loc doesn't read newspapers; he prefers to read the classical Chinese stories of chivalry and adventure that are popular in Viet Nam. He and his friends talk about their families and their romantic escapades rather than about the war. Loc knew of President Diem and had nothing against him, but he didn't like what he heard about Diem's relatives, especially his sister-in-law, Madame Nhu. He didn't care about Diem's overthrow, because he figured that he would still be a soldier, regardless of who was leading the country. He kept up with the heads of government after Diem for a while, but he doesn't know who is in power now. Loc believes Ho Chi Minh is a general in North Viet Nam; he is not familiar with the names of a single Viet Cong or American, and he knows very little about the United States. Loc, a Buddhist who goes to pagoda on the first and fifteenth of the month if he is not out on an operation, is under the impression that most Americans are Roman Catholics. He thinks that American soldiers are in South Viet Nam to help the government fight the VC because the government is too weak to fight them alone. He mistakenly believes that all the American soldiers in South Viet Nam are volunteers. There are a few American soldiers advising his battalion. They have never talked to Loc, not because he can't speak English—the Americans have interpreters—but because the Americans never speak to privates. Loc doesn't know why the war began, or how it could have been avoided. He knows the country is partitioned; he doesn't know who is responsible and he has never heard of the Geneva Agreements. He doesn't know how long the war will last—"I'm not a fortuneteller"—but he doesn't expect it to be over next week. He believes his side will come out victorious in the end, and that it has a much better chance of winning now than it did in 1962, because of the American build-up and because people dislike the Viet Cong more than they used to. "The VC know we can call for an airstrike any time, and now they often run away from us," he says. "People are complaining that the Viet Cong interfere in their lives and that it's because of the VC that there is artillery shelling and bombing. People hate the Viet Cong more than before, but of course people in completely VC-controlled areas can't afford to hate the VC." Even if the Viet Cong are blamed, Loc is against the bombing of hamlets in South Viet Nam—though he approves of the bombing of VC bases—because he has seen many innocent women and children killed by artillery and airstrikes. He favors the bombing of North Viet Nam, to prevent the North Vietnamese from sending in troops and weapons, and to force them to withdraw their troops from South Viet Nam. He thinks when his side wins the war, the VC should be jailed and reeducated. He would like to see his country reunified, but he doesn't know how it can be done.

Loc doesn't like the Viet Cong because they interfere with people's lives, because they have confiscated some of his relatives' land and distributed it to other people, and because their mines and roadblocks restrict his freedom of movement; he objects to this particularly when he is on his way to see his wife and children. He doesn't think the VC are Communists or traitors, but simply opportunists who would like to run the country. He accepts the fact that he must fight them, but no one has ever told him exactly why he is fighting. When his company is busy on operations, the soldiers receive no indoctrination whatsoever. When they are not too busy, the company's officers, or officers from regimental headquarters, give them a lecture every couple of months. "The lecturers talk about all kinds of things, like government policy and military discipline," Loc says. "From time to time, they tell us about Communism and they ask us why we should fight the Viet Cong. None of us answers—it's not compulsory to answer—and they don't even bother to answer themselves. We are soldiers, and if we're not fighting, we like to be free to go out and have a good time. We'd rather not sit around at a dull lecture." In their leisure time, Loc and his friends receive no additional military training. Loc wishes he would be given training as a mechanic while he is in the Army, but becoming a mechanic after the war is a pipedream, like winning the national lottery, and living in Saigon. He knows the Army offers no such training and he would be perfectly content to take up his work in the rice fields in his native hamlet when the war ends.

"I haven't got much against my military life," Loc says. "It's a hard life, but I'm used to it. I guess I feel unhappy only when I'm still plodding in the jungle under the rain and I'm hungry; when I'm back from the operation, I feel all right again. The only thing I really mind about the Army is the lack of freedom. I very rarely feel sick, but what I don't like is that if I have a headache I still have to go out and fight. If I'm well, I certainly don't mind going out to fight. It's a man's duty. We all know when we go out that some of us may not come back, but we're not afraid of dying. We are accustomed to death. I think the whole company's morale is very high when we win, especially when we can lay our hands on VC weapons, but the company's morale doesn't go down when someone is killed. I haven't seen any reason for the morale of the whole unit to go down. An individual soldier's morale is likely to go down when his family is in trouble and he can't get a few days off. As a regular, I'm in the Army until the war is over—there's no question of getting out while there is still fighting. I've heard that many soldiers desert from the Army, though I've never known any deserters. I couldn't be a deserter. Of course, if there were an honorable way to get out of the Army tomorrow, I would. That's one of my greatest wishes. That's what we all wish."

»»»» IX ««««

>>>>> *Huynh Van Kim*, who has also used the aliases Huynh Thanh and Huynh Long, joined the Viet Cong in January, 1958, when it was still known as the underground revolutionary movement. He was then twenty-one years old.

One night in December, 1957, a dozen Viet Cong recruiting agents appeared in his hamlet in Binh Thuan village, in the delta province of Dinh Tuong. Some of the agents, who were dressed as Viet Minh troops, were armed. They invited Kim and five or six other young men in the hamlet to accompany them to a base in the jungle a mile away. Kim was afraid and said he wouldn't go, but the agents told him they just wanted to have a friendly talk with him and he consented to follow them. Once at their base, the agents lectured the boys. The lectures pointed out some of the shortcomings of Diem's régime—his failure to hold the agreed-upon 1956 elections, to carry out land reform, or to remove corrupt officials. The young men were urged to join the revolutionary movement in order to work for Diem's overthrow. The agents said that this would result

149

in justice for the people, a more equitable distribution of land, and reunification of the country. After a couple of hours, the agents let the boys go, warning them to say nothing about their activities. The agents returned every night. Each time they came to the hamlet they invited five or six young men to go with them. They came to Kim's home and invited him to lectures every third or fourth night. The agents kept asking him if he had made a decision to join the movement. At the end of a month of lectures, Kim agreed to join.

Kim, who is now a well-built, high-strung, chain-smoking young man of twenty-nine with watchful eyes, a forced smile, and a nervous habit of cracking his knuckles, joined the Viet Cong for several reasons. He was favorably impressed by the VC indoctrination lectures; he didn't personally know of the injustices the agents mentioned—he thought his hamlet chief was all right, his grandfather owned several acres of land, and he had never heard a word about any elections—but he had no way of determining whether the injustices existed elsewhere, and the agents were so persuasive that he believed them. Kim was most eager for reunification. Many of his cousins, Viet Minh who had fought against the French, had gone north with their units in 1954, and he and their families missed them. If the country were whole again, they might return. The fact that two of Kim's older brothers had been killed by the Viet Minh while serving in the French Army left him with no ill feelings toward the Viet Minh. French troops had come to Binh Thuan on operations and had done a great deal of raping and stealing in the village. He thought his brothers would never have joined the French Army if they had seen

French soldiers burn down their own parents' home, as Kim had. According to Kim, fear also played a part in his decision to join the Viet Cong. "I wasn't forced to join," he says, "but I felt a veiled threat, because the government seemed pretty indifferent or helpless to prevent the armed agents from coming into my village and taking people away for indoctrination." Kim also joined because he had no appealing alternative. He was the ninth of eleven children. Three of his brothers and sisters died of illness, in addition to the two brothers killed by the Viet Minh; Kim, two older sisters, one older brother, and two younger brothers survived. There was no primary school in Kim's hamlet. He started primary school in another hamlet in Binh Thuan village when he was twelve. He enjoyed school very much (mathematics was the subject he liked most, dictation the subject he liked least), but the road to school was flooded most of the time, making attendance difficult, and he gave up school after four years, and went to work in his grandfather's rice fields. He didn't care for the work. The VC also promised Kim he could stay near his village if he joined them, and he believed that if he was drafted into the government Army, he would be sent far from home. Kim had married a girl from another hamlet in Binh Thuan when he was eighteen. He had seen her at school and at the village market. Kim's father, a schoolteacher, had deserted the family when Kim was fourteen and had gone to live in another hamlet in the village with his mistress; Kim asked his mother to get the girl for him and she did. They had been happy together during the first three years of their marriage and had one son. Kim wanted to remain near his wife.

151

The day after Kim announced his decision, the agents took him to another nearby jungle base, which consisted of several well-concealed thatched huts on the bank of a creek. About thirty people, all of them South Vietnamese, lived there—ten armed senior agents and twenty newly recruited junior agents, who were not given arms. From the day they arrived at the base, Kim and the other new junior agents followed the same rigorous daily schedule—seven and a half hours of political studies, an hour and a half of physical exercise, and an hour of social life, which was devoted to learning revolutionary poems and songs. They were fed three skimpy meals a day, of rice and fish, or just rice and salt. At the political lectures, the senior agents dwelt on the evils of the Saigon government. The government was blamed over and over again for countless injustices, and for the partition of the country. The lectures were followed by discussions of the ideas that had just been repeated for hours. "During the first month, I only listened to the lecturers," Kim says. "I didn't take part in the discussions. Then I got more interested, and I also realized that it didn't pay to keep silent, so I decided to be more talkative and to show more enthusiasm. I got through the initial period of political studies in two months. For those who didn't seem as receptive to the ideas as I was, political studies lasted as long as five or six months." The lecturers told Kim, a nominal Buddhist, not to believe in the Buddha.

In March, 1958, Kim was given two hand grenades. He was assigned to escort senior agents on their nightly recruiting excursions to the villages in the area. He was supposed to help protect them and to master their recruiting technique. He still attended political lectures, but only for an hour or two a day. In November, 1959, as a result of having effectively escorted the senior agents and of having done well in his political training, he was made a cadre and became a senior recruiting agent. He was proud to be promoted. In early 1960, Kim was told of the imminent formation of a nationwide Liberation Front. He was also told that the revolutionary movement would soon become more militant. He continued his nightly recruiting missions and his daily political studies and he was also given a little military training: he was taught how to fire, dismantle, and reassemble an old French bolt-action rifle. In his first two years with the VC, Kim saw his family only infrequently, at night, when he was on his way to a recruiting mission near his home. He was too busy in the daytime, studying or sleeping, and visits home were discouraged by his superiors. Although the food was bad and Kim had to ask his family for clothes and spending money (the VC weren't paid and were taught to regard the government soldiers as mercenaries) he was happy with his work.

On December 1, 1960, the sixty people at the base, some of them young men Kim had recruited, were divided into two groups. Thirty, including Kim, were assigned to the military section, thirty, to the political section. They were carefully primed by the senior agents for a night attack on Binh Thuan that was to take place in mid-December. On the appointed night, both sections went together to Kim's native village. The political section had a few weapons, but their main duty was to shout slogans and declarations, urging people to rise up against the government. The military team's duty was to kill certain pre-selected government officials and supporters in the village. The VC took the village completely by surprise. They had several guns, but they didn't fire a shot. They used scimitars to behead ten people in the seven hamlets in the village, including the chief of Kim's hamlet. Kim didn't kill his hamlet chief, but he killed five of the other victims, three men and two women. "It was the first time I'd done any killing, but it didn't upset me," he says. "Before we decided to kill those people, we discussed their misdeeds at length, and we had official documents to prove their guilt. The women were spies. I personally found out that they had hung up torches to warn government troops of our presence in the village when we came to recruit." That night, the government troops fired at the VC from a nearby outpost. They didn't hit any of them. After the attack, the VC returned to their jungle base.

Over the next year, Kim went on recruiting expeditions and also accompanied some of his comrades to villages in the area to assassinate government officials and soldiers, and to capture badly needed weapons. At that time, the VC at the base were poorly armed, but in most villages there was only one platoon of government militia, which couldn't protect an entire village. Government troops in nearby outposts became reluctant to leave their forts after they had been ambushed a few times when they had set out to rescue a hamlet. Occasionally, the VC clashed with government soldiers out on patrol. In one skirmish, two Viet Cong were killed and Kim was wounded; a rifle bullet grazed his right knee. He was able to run about half a mile, and then had to be carried the rest of the way back to the base by his comrades. It took his wound two weeks to heal. In 1961, fifteen VC were killed; their losses were more than made up for by new recruits from the terrorized villages. That year, the VC at Kim's base killed about fifteen government officials and soldiers, and captured a number of guns. At the end of 1961, Kim was made a political cadre and was assigned to work with the youth in Binh Thuan. He gave them political education (while continuing his own political studies) and incited them to destroy bridges, tear up roads, and demonstrate against the government.

In January, 1963, Kim was sent to a VC district headquarters near Binh Thuan. He stayed there a while and it was decided that he would be promoted from village guerrilla to the main force Viet Cong, on the basis of his good record. Kim was unhappy with this promotion. In the last five years, he had been able to spend very little time with his family, although he had never lived far from his hamlet. In 1962, his wife had left him and had returned to her father's home. Their son was living with Kim's mother. Kim wanted to be near his village, as he'd been promised when he joined the VC, so that he could see his child, but he was afraid to protest. He was sent to join a main force unit in Tay Ninh, another province in the delta. It took Kim nearly two months to make the trip from Binh Thuan to a jungle camp a short distance from the provincial capital of Tay Ninh, a distance of only seventy-five miles. He and his companions walked at night and had to check with local Viet Cong officials every step of the way. He reached his destination in early May, and was granted a week's rest. For the next six months, he was given his first real military training. He was taught to handle recoilless and automatic rifles, machine and submachine guns, carbines, and mortars. Kim was allowed to fire only one round of ammunition during his whole training period. He was told to shoot at a mark on the side of a deserted government outpost, from a distance of two hundred yards. He came close to the target and was considered a good marksman. The second time he fired was in actual combat. During his military training period, Kim spent an hour and a half a day on political studies. "In the late fifties, we were taught to fight against the national government, but after 1961, the one point driven home to us more than any other was the need to drive the American imperialists out of South Viet Nam," he says. "We were told to attack them at every opportunity, to keep them from taking over our country." In October, 1963, Kim was assigned to a main force battalion stationed in Tay Ninh province. He became a mortar crewman and had his first chance to fire the mortar on the night of November 1, 1963, when his battalion attacked a government outpost in a nearby province. Over the following months, Kim's battalion attacked a number of other government outposts, most of them in Tay Ninh province, and got into several minor and two major clashes with government troops. In February, 1964, when Kim's battalion was attacking an outpost in Tay Ninh, ten of his comrades were killed. Kim and four other VC were wounded. A bullet grazed Kim's thigh, but it didn't hit a bone and he required no surgery. The Viet Cong considered this a major engagement and a victory, because they overran the outpost. In the second major clash, in July, 1964—the biggest action Kim has ever taken part in—his battalion attacked another outpost in Tay Ninh and ambushed a government relief column. The fighting went on sporadically for two days and two nights. One hundred VC were killed and fifty wounded. Fifty government troops were killed and the battle was considered a defeat. "Practically all of our casualties were inflicted by bombers and armored personnel carriers," Kim says. "The airpower was so terrible we couldn't overrun the outpost and seize any weapons. With airpower, the VC could give the Army a much rougher time."

When they weren't fighting, Kim and the men in his battalion spent their time attending political lectures, receiving additional military training, and collecting provisions from the villages in the area. They sometimes slept at battalion headquarters, sometimes in VC villages, and sometimes, when traveling, in the jungle in hammocks. "It was especially uncomfortable when it was raining," Kim says. "We often had to work too hard when we were badly fed. But I liked the spirit of democracy and that made up for many things. We were free to criticize any officials or commanders, no matter how important they were, and they had to admit their shortcomings and promise to do better in the future. We didn't have to fear criticizing people. We were criticized often ourselves. Criticism sessions were held once a week."

At the end of August, 1964, Kim's mother came to Tay Ninh to see him. She begged him to leave the Viet Cong. Kim's older brother and one of his younger brothers were still in Binh Thuan, working in the rice fields, but one of his younger brothers had gone to Saigon to study and had become a government policeman. Kim's mother was in tears when she told Kim she wanted her sons on one side. "I'd been having serious doubts about the VC and I wanted very much to be stationed back home again, but if my mother hadn't come to see me, I would have kept my rebellious ideas to myself," Kim says. "I felt very sorry when I saw my mother weeping. I began saying I wanted to go home, and I was severely criticized at the criticism sessions for being selfish. One day, I lost my temper. I almost shot a man who had criticized me especially sharply. As a result, I was sent to a reeducation center for recalcitrant elements, in September, 1964." At the VC reeducation center in Tay Ninh province, Kim and forty other "recalcitrant elements" spent their time listening to political lectures and doing a few other chores, such as growing vegetables and building huts. They didn't have to fight. "During the first months, I couldn't help showing my resentment," Kim says. "I realized that wasn't getting me anywhere, so after a while I began to pose as a docile element and to master the lectures. After a few months, I was asked whether I wanted to continue with the Front or rejoin my family. I knew this was a test. No one is allowed to retire from the VC until he's very old, very sick, or seriously disabled. I was afraid to arouse suspicion, so I said I wanted to continue. They sent me out on several food-buying missions. I didn't try to escape, because I knew I was being watched closely. I was released from the reeducation center in July, 1965, and sent to a different regiment in Tay Ninh, to wait for a new assignment. The regiment was based in the jungle, very close to the Cambodian border." While waiting, Kim was sent out on various missions. Once, he was sent to a village about five miles from the regimental base to tell the village cadres to take special care to prevent defections, because the government was going to drop leaflets over the village describing its "Open Arms" program in the next few days. According to the government, Viet Cong who surrendered would receive amnesty under the Open Arms program. The cadres were told to tell the VC that the program was a hoax, and that the government would torture defectors to death. Kim's regimental headquarters had received word of the imminent leaflet drop from VC infiltrated into the Open Arms program. Kim was often dispatched on food-buying missions. One day in August, 1965, he and three comrades were sent to a village a few miles from regimental headquarters to buy rice and fish. Dried fish was not available in the large quantity they had been ordered to get. Kim's friends returned to regimental headquarters in the afternoon, with the provisions they had succeeded in purchasing. Kim stayed on in the village to try to buy more fish. He spent the night under the watchful eyes of the local VC agents. The following day, there was a government operation in the village. The local VC cadres had to flee, so the tight VC control system was temporarily relaxed. Kim had been looking for an opportunity to defect from the Viet Cong. He decided that this was an excellent moment, because no one was watching him. He went to a farming area at the foot of the Black Lady mountain, where peasants were working in the rice fields under the protection of a government outpost. He stayed with the peasants until four in the afternoon, and then boarded a civilian bus with them. The bus took him to the provincial capital of Tay Ninh. When he arrived there, he asked his way to a police station. At the Tay Ninh police station, Kim told officials he had been a VC for seven and a half years, and had decided to defect to the government side. He asked for amnesty under the Open Arms program.

Kim had wanted to leave the Viet Cong ever since his

transfer to the main forces in early 1963. He was tired of fighting. He had killed over fifteen people in addition to those he had killed in his village in December, 1960. He feared that he would be killed himself in the stepped-up fighting. He had also become disillusioned with the VC. "I was enthusiastic about the Viet Cong during my first years," Kim says. "I couldn't continue school, or do anything else I wanted to do, and I didn't like working in the rice fields. The VC seemed to be the only good chance I had to advance. When I was recruited, I was told that we would win in two years, and that all the people would be happy and the country reunified. After 1962, the prospect of victory and reunification grew dimmer, because the government was reinforced with American weapons and men. I was most enthusiastic about the Viet Cong in 1962, before my wife left me, when we were doing well and victory seemed to be in sight. Then I began to realize we might have to fight for years to reach the target we had thought within our easy reach. By early 1965, I even thought we might lose, if the Americans stuck it out in Viet Nam. We were told the Americans wouldn't stick it out, but we had been told in 1964 that the Americans wouldn't dare bomb North Viet Nam, and we knew that they eventually did. We also learned that the higher VC casualty figures were being hidden from us. It's true that our political education was intensive, but only fresh recruits believed entirely in what they were told. That's why most of the Front's real achievements are made by the young. People who have been with the Front for some time have had opportunities to test their side's assets. They come to realize that a good deal of what the political commissars taught was questionable. Many men who have been with the Front for a long time become dissatisfied and want to return to their families, but they don't act on their dissatisfaction. They are afraid, and they realize that once they've been in the Viet Cong, they don't have much of a future out of it. Many VC officials are really dedicated. They control the others, and push them to get things done. I probably would never have gotten started on the road to defection if my mother hadn't come to see me in Tay Ninh. I didn't like to see her weeping."

When he arrived at the police station in Tay Ninh and said he wanted to defect and get amnesty, Kim gave the officials there some Viet Cong papers—his purchasing orders for the dried fish—to prove his case. The officials kept him at the police station for three days and three nights. During that time, he underwent two four-hour-long sessions of questioning. He was asked about the activities and whereabouts of certain VC units, and was asked to give the names of high-ranking VC officers under whom he had served. Since many VC had aliases (Kim was called Huynh Thanh as a Viet Cong village guerrilla, Huynh Long when he was transferred to the main forces) he didn't know how helpful the names he supplied would be. After three days, he was taken to the Open Arms center in Tay Ninh, where he spent two weeks undergoing several more sessions similar to the ones at the police station. He was then taken by helicopter to a military compound at Bien Hoa, the headquarters of the third Army corps, which was in charge of Tay Ninh province, where he was interrogated for another two weeks. His questioners were very nice to him and were the first people since his defection to ask him about his personal life. They offered to help him find a job when he had gone through the Open Arms program. In September, Kim was sent to a military installation in Saigon—he had never been in the capital until then—and he spent almost a month there undergoing two long sessions of questioning every day, except Sunday. His interrogators, three Army intelligence officers, asked him to give them information about units he had been with, and about other units in the delta with which he was familiar. "I was treated badly by those officers," Kim says. "They always insisted I was telling them lies. They often beat me with a small stick, slapped my face, and insulted me. They asked me what a certain VC regiment did, and I told them it was a logistics and supply regiment. They beat me and told me they knew it was an important fighting regiment. It wasn't. The ARVN has more troops and better equipment than the VC—the VC fight in sandals, the ARVN soldiers have boots—but ARVN intelligence is very poor. The ARVN would be more effective if it had intelligence like the VC's. The Viet Cong have agents everywhere, from peasants in hamlets to high-ranking Army officers in Saigon. I've never seen evidence that the ARVN has infiltrated the VC." In October, Kim was abruptly taken to an Open Arms center in Saigon, a cluster of buildings with dormitories accommodating about a hundred defectors. Upon arrival at the center, Kim was given three hundred piasters. Each subsequent day, he has been given eighteen piasters, six for each meal. He usually skips breakfast and uses six piasters for cigarettes instead; he spent the three hundred original piasters on cigarettes, too. During his first six weeks at the Open Arms center, Kim followed a schedule similar to the one he had followed when he first joined the Viet Cong; it included six and a half hours of indoctrination a day. "I've been treated well, and I've been eating better on two meals here than I did in the Viet Cong on three," Kim says. "The living conditions are fine, but the VC political education seemed much more interesting to me. VC lecturers are very articulate. They use concrete words, which appeal to me. VC lecturers are South Vietnamese. The lecturers at the center were born in North Viet Nam and in the central part of South Viet Nam. They speak with a different accent than I do, and they expound too many abstract ideas. They confuse me. They talk about the history of Viet Nam, the fallacies of Communism, and the aggressive activities of Communism in the world. I cannot grasp what they mean, because everything is too general. At the center, we can feel very much at ease and we can afford to be absent-minded. I had to be very attentive at VC lectures and I had to repeat the ideas all the time. If I were a lecturer, I would enforce the Viet Cong's harsh policy. A teacher has to be strict to drive ideas into students' heads. I think the system at the center is much too relaxed, and it's very difficult for students to master ideas. The lecturers keep on talking about the revolutionary war council and its revolutionary policy, but they haven't told us who's in charge of the government. A few people got so bored with the aimless lectures that they just took off. The security is very loose. I could have escaped if I had wanted to."

Kim has had time to think a few things over since finishing the six weeks indoctrination course at the Open Arms center in Saigon. He used to believe that the United States wanted to take over South Viet Nam to get its minerals, forests, and rice, as he had been told by the VC. He no longer believes this. He thinks the United States is so prosperous that the Americans do not need anything in Viet Nam. He now believes individual people in the United States are good; he has a few reservations about the American government, because he thinks it is making people demonstrate against the war in Viet Nam. "I don't think the demonstrators are sincere," Kim says. "I think they're tools of the United States government. The American government cooks up the demonstrations to cover its real intentions. It is trying to mislead Hanoi into thinking the United States will pull out of Viet Nam while it is actually escalating the war. It's not good for a government to do this." Kim was against all bombing when he was in the Viet Cong, but now he says he is in favor of bombing North Viet Nam and VC bases in the south. "But I'm against bombing South Vietnamese hamlets, even if there are VC in them," he says. "If you want to get the support of the general population, you have to work on the political front. You shouldn't kill people and destroy their property. If you do that, the people will get dissatisfied with you and the Viet Cong will have a good chance of getting the support of those who live through the bombing." Kim used to think the VC would win the war. He now believes the government will win, as long as the Americans don't withdraw (and he doesn't think they will) and as long as the Americans and the government forces are fighting only VC and North Vietnamese troops. "I think the government side would win, even if the Communist Chinese sent troops," Kim says. "Numbers don't mean anything, and the Chinese are quite backward in weaponry. But if the Soviet Union became deeply involved, to the extent of sending troops, the Russians would win, because they would only get involved if they really understood the war. The Russians have had much more experience in international wars than the Americans. In 1945, the Russians liberated Germany and launched the world-wide Socialism drive. They've had more practice helping people fight for a cause. The Russians are also much more advanced in technology than the Americans. They were the first to send up spaceships. But they won't send troops, because the Russians and the Chinese don't get along well, and the Chinese won't let them."

When Kim leaves the Open Arms center in Saigon in a short while, he will go to Bien Hoa, where the authorities who interrogated him there have promised to help him find a job. He hopes his mother and his son will be able to join him in Bien Hoa. His wife has remarried. He does not blame her for anything, but he still loves her. He would like to remarry, but he doesn't know if he will be able to, because he expects difficult days ahead financially. Kim knows he must stay in a city. He wouldn't be safe from the VC in the countryside, or in a small district town. Kim doesn't speak English, and he doesn't think he will be able to find a decent job. "My prospects don't look too good," Kim says. "I'm grateful to the government. I've been nicely treated since I left the Viet Cong. But I would still like to go to school and I'll never be able to. The VC are right in saying that there are no real opportunities for poor people in this country. I feel a little bit sorry about having killed so many people, but my conscience is pretty much at peace, because I acted under conviction. I often wonder if I'll ever find anything to believe in again. I've spent so much of my time in the jungle that I don't think I'm good for anything now anyway. When I first left the Viet Cong, I worried what would happen to me if they won the war. I don't place as much value on my life now as I did then. I'm no longer afraid of dying. I don't think the VC infiltrators in the Open Arms program will kill me. I'm not worth it. But if they do—well, if I die today, I won't have to die tomorrow."

X

>>>>>> *Nguyen Ngoc Vinh* is a North Vietnamese soldier. He was drafted into the People's Army of the Democratic Republic of Viet Nam in April, 1962. After serving in the North for three years, Vinh volunteered to go south to fight, and he infiltrated into South Viet Nam in the summer of 1965. At the end of January, 1966, during a skirmish with some South Vietnamese troops, he was hit in both arms by rifle bullets and taken prisoner. Vinh is now being held at an interrogation center in Saigon, along with forty other North Vietnamese soldiers of the four hundred who have been captured since the war began. He is a tough young man, sturdy for a Vietnamese, with a nervous twitch in his eyes, a ready smile, and a forthright manner.

Vinh was born in February, 1938, in a hamlet in Thanh Hoa province. His parents died when he was about five years old, and he does not remember them. He has been told that they were poor peasants, who cultivated a tiny patch of riceland they owned. Vinh's father also collected wood to help support his family. Vinh's father served in the French colonial Army many years ago, but in the nineteen-thirties he joined the Indo-Chinese Communist Party, which in 1941 initiated the formation of the Viet Minh. His activities in the underground resistance were discovered by the French, and he spent three years in prison not long before his death.

After his parents died, Vinh, an older brother, and an older sister—there were only the three children in the family—went to stay with aunts and uncles who lived in the same hamlet. The three helped out with their relatives' children, animals, and household chores. When Vinh was thirteen, his older brother married, and he went to live with his brother and started working in the rice fields of one of the prosperous peasants in the hamlet.

While Vinh was growing up, land in what is now North Viet Nam was privately owned. Most peasants in the North owned the small pieces of land they tilled, but there were also some relatively wealthy landowners, who had fifty or sixty acres, and some very poor peasants, who were landless. (Land was much more unevenly distributed in the Mekong delta area of what is now South Viet Nam, where two and a half per cent of the landowners held forty-five per cent of the arable land.) In late 1953, the Vietnamese Communist Party announced a Land Reform Campaign. The real objective of the campaign was not a more equitable distribution of land; it was the destruction of the traditional Vietnamese rural society. The great majority of Vietnamese lived in the countryside, and the Communists were intent on creating a new rural society, amenable to their rule. The land question was the vehicle whereby this revolutionary process was to be achieved.

Early in 1954, during the first stage of the Land Reform

Campaign, Party cadres divided villagers into categories; the peasants were classified as very poor (landless), poor, middle, and rich, and the landlords occupied a category by themselves. In many villages, there were no actual landlords, and in these some of the more prosperous landowning peasants were simply called landlords. Any who attempted to escape this designation by giving their land to the state were not allowed to do so. They were forced to remain landlords, because their existence was the excuse for the entire process. At first, the landlords—the richest, and therefore the most "reactionary," residents of the village—were simply made to pay heavy fines for excess rents they were said to have charged their tenant farmers in the past. At the same time, the poorest peasants in the village were indoctrinated by special Land Reform cadres, some of whom had been trained in Communist China, where land reform had been carried out a few years earlier. These peasants were made to attend a special course in Crimes Committed by the Landowning Class, in which they were taught how the landlords had, over the years, exploited, cheated, and oppressed them. The peasants subsequently charged the landlords with assorted "crimes" at well-staged denunciation sessions. That many of the charges—for example, landlords having poisoned wells, raped women, and drowned children—were demonstrably untrue, and that many of the accused were not actually landlords was irrelevant. The denounced landlords were then judged by Special People's Tribunals. A minimum number of death sentences per village had been fixed by the Party in advance, and some landlords were publicly shot; others were sentenced to long terms at hard labor in prison camps.

171

The second stage of the Land Reform Campaign, which began late in 1954—after the Communist Party had extended its authority over all of North Viet Nam, as a result of the Geneva Agreements—was more severe than the first in every respect. Having eliminated the larger landowners and the other people whom it deemed most likely to resist its rule, the Party widened the attack to complete the forcible dismantling of the village society. The population was reclassified, and many persons who had previously been designated as middle or rich peasants were now called landlords and were treated accordingly. Landlords were not merely fined; their land and most of their belongings were confiscated and redistributed among the landless peasants. The Party quotas of death sentences and prison terms for landlords were raised to five times what they had been. By mid-1956, the Land Reform Campaign had developed into a purge on a national scale. The arbitrary trials, the indignities heaped on selected victims, and the brutal executions had created an atmosphere of insecurity and civil disorder in the villages. There was growing hostility toward the Party and its cadres. Many of the people who had been shot or imprisoned as landlords were members of prosperous peasant families who had joined the Party from motives of patriotism or political ambition in the early years of the struggle against the French; as part of the general effort to establish a proletarian dictatorship in the countryside, the Party leadership was intent on ousting these old members and creating a new hard core of village cadres, drawn from the landless peasantry.

In August, 1956, Ho Chi Minh announced that "errors" had been committed in the Land Reform Campaign, and promised that they would be rectified. The terror had deliberately been allowed to reach excessive proportions in order to insure the rending of the village social fabric, and now the Party leadership, having decided that the campaign had gone far enough, was eager to dispel the animosity that it had aroused and to restore an atmosphere of normality to the villages. In the Rectification of Errors Campaign that followed, thousands of persons who had been sent to prison because of purported "misclassification," including twelve thousand former Party members, were released and allowed to return home. These and other measures, however, were not enough to avert violence in the aftermath of the Land Reform Campaign. In many villages, the newly released prisoners clashed with the people who had been responsible for their imprisonment, and there were widespread instances of murder and assault. A number of peasant revolts against the Communist authorities broke out. Ironically, the biggest revolt took place in Ho Chi Minh's native province, Nghe An, not far from his birthplace. In early November, 1956, a well-armed division of North Vietnamese troops fought twenty thousand peasants of Nghe An, who were armed with sharpened staves and other crude weapons. Six thousand peasants were killed or were deported to remote areas, and soldiers were billeted in dissident villages. In an effort to transfer the peasants' hatred from the Party to its individual cadres, the Party as a whole made scapegoats of certain Land Reform Campaign officials.

When the peasant revolts had been suppressed and some sense of calm had been more or less restored to the countryside, the Party began the final stage of the Land

Reform Campaign—the progressive abolition of private ownership. The landless peasants who had received the land and possessions of the people designated as landlords were now taxed severely as a demonstration that private ownership was no longer feasible in the new society. By 1958, much of the land in North Viet Nam had been quietly collectivized, and agricultural cooperatives had been established. At first, the cooperatives were small. As their membership grew, thanks to the prohibitive taxation of privately owned plots, to intensive political indoctrination, and to other pressures, they merged. In Vinh's village, there are now two cooperatives; in some villages there is only one. About ninety per cent of North Viet Nam's rural population belongs to cooperatives.

Estimates of the number of persons who died during the Land Reform Campaign—including those who were shot, those who died in prisons and labor camps as a result of the bad conditions, those who committed suicide, and members of landlords' families (mostly small children) who died of starvation as a result of ostracism by the villagers—range from fifty thousand to five hundred thousand. Vinh was too young to play an active role in the Land Reform Campaign, but he witnessed the landlord-denunciation sessions in his village and the shooting of two landlords. "Both landlords deserved to be shot, from what I heard," he says. "One was not only a landlord but also a bad official, and the other was charged with being a spy for the French." Vinh does not know that many people were condemned as French spies simply because someone testified they had once been seen waving at a French airplane. Vinh and his relatives were classified as poor peasants, and so were in no danger during the campaign. He is unaware that many thousands of people in his country were killed in the campaign, because he doesn't know what went on outside his district. Travel in North Viet Nam has long been restricted—anyone who wants to spend the night in another village or go to another province must have a pass—and the newspapers print only what the régime decides will enlighten the public. For the same reasons, Vinh does not know of the uprising in Nghe An; he has heard only vague reports of small rebellions in a few scattered areas. He thinks of the Land Reform Campaign and its repercussions as ancient history. "After the Rectification of Errors Campaign, no one had any grievances," he says. "The policy was right. The Party's policy is never wrong. Only the people in charge of carrying it out were bad. The Rectification of Errors Campaign made everything fine." Vinh himself is opposed to the use of terrorism. "We've learned from our mistakes," he says. "As soon as we liberate the South, we'll carry out land reform, but no landlords will be killed. We'll try to reeducate them." Vinh says he has never been given any information about the Viet Cong. In reply to allegations that they practice terrorism in the South, and in the past nine years have assassinated thousands of government officials, school teachers, medical personnel, social workers, and peasants who have opposed them, he says merely, "I'm not in a position to know such things."

Vinh belonged to one of his village cooperatives before he was drafted, and all his relatives at home belong to one. At the end of every working day in the rice fields, the members of the cooperative are graded by the cadres according to how well they have worked. There are two rice harvests a year, and after each one the members are paid, in rice, on the basis of the marks they have received. Good workers may receive more rice than they need to feed their families, and they are permitted to sell the surplus. The few people who have not joined a cooperative, preferring to till their own land, usually earn more than any of the members do, but have to pay higher prices for some items in the government stores. "People in the cooperatives and people outside them come out the same materially, but members of the cooperatives have certain advantages," Vinh says. "The people outside them have to fend for themselves all the time. The people in them are taken care of—even during the bad months just before the harvest is in, when they've run out of rice. They can borrow from the cooperative. They also have a sense of comradeship and of collective achievement. There are still a few people who haven't reconciled themselves to the idea of cooperatives, but there are fewer all the time, because the government has made it clear that free enterprise always leads to economic discrepancy and social injustice."

Rice and meat are rationed in North Viet Nam, and many people must supplement their diets with sweet potatoes, corn, and cassava, which are readily available but not very popular. Flower-printed cloth can be purchased in unlimited quantities, but Vietnamese peasants have little use for flowered cloth. The solid-color cloth that is used for everyday clothes is rationed to four or five yards a year per person. Cooperative members aren't allowed to own buffalos and oxen; these essential means of production have been collectivized. They may use their free time, however, to raise and sell pigs and chickens, and thus earn additional cash income. With the money they can buy such unrationed items as domestic cigarettes, soft drinks, beer, Russian-made wristwatches, and Chinese-manufactured pens. "The standard of living in the North isn't ideal, but it's improving," Vinh says.

Most people in the countryside live in sparsely furnished thatched huts. Even simple furniture is rather expensive. As for calendars, which can be found on the walls of even the poorest peasant huts in South Viet Nam, they are considered a real luxury in the North. Instead, pictures of Ho Chi Minh are hung in the majority of the Northern homes. "Calendars are more expensive than pictures of President Ho," Vinh says. "Anyway, it's better to have a picture of Ho Chi Minh than a calendar, because President Ho's picture has more meaning, and he's much more decorative than a calendar."

Vinh's major occupation before he became a soldier was working in the rice fields. When he was not in the fields, the cadres kept him and the other villagers busy with so-called "collective activities." Among these, at certain times of the year, was repair work on roads and dikes —compulsory, unpaid drudgery that was called *corvée* labor under the French colonial system but is now known by the socially approved term of civilian labor. Vinh never went to school as a child. Before going into the Army, he learned to read and write by attending free adult literacy courses, and he also received fifteen months of medical training, qualifying him to work part time—and without pay—as a male nurse who was permitted to treat common ailments. He was a member of the youth organization, the cooperative organization, and the village militia. One important activity

of each of these organizations was holding sessions of criticism and self-criticism. This fringe benefit of life in a
Socialist society allowed Vinh and his fellow-villagers, while
publicly denouncing their own faults, to castigate everyone
else's, too. "In a criticism session, I am permitted to criticize
anyone, no matter what his rank," Vinh says. "I'm free to
criticize the board of directors of the cooperative, the village
administrators, the police, and the political instructors, even
though most of them are Party members." Vinh was once
accused of giving a patient an overdose of medicine, and
once criticized himself for occasionally using his work as a
male nurse as a pretext to shirk less pleasant obligations.
"In the French days, we had no political equality," Vinh
says. "Officials tyrannized over the people, who were helpless, for they had no recourse to anyone. Now officials must
act as the people's servants, not as their bosses. It's possible
for us to ask for the dismissal of any official we don't like.
Outside the criticism sessions, of course, we have to obey
all our superiors, and we are not supposed to go around complaining about things."

The Viet Minh gained control of Vinh's area in the fall
of 1945, when he was seven years old, and they held it
throughout the First Indo-China War. The French bombed
the area heavily, but Vinh cannot remember ever seeing any
French troops or administrators. He owes his ideas about
political inequality under the French to another important
activity of the organizations to which he belonged—"political-education" sessions. Each of the organizations held
such sessions, and the evils of capitalism and imperialism were a favorite subject of all of them. Vinh was told
that capitalists always tried to seize weak countries, in order

to open new markets and to exploit natural resources for their own benefit. They never industrialized the invaded countries or raised their living standards; they wanted the people in those unfortunate places to remain enslaved forever. In the nineteen-forties and early nineteen-fifties, the political sessions dwelt exclusively on the Vietnamese experience under the French. Vinh has never heard a good word about the French. He considers his area lucky because no Frenchmen set foot in it during the First Indo-China War; he has seen children of mixed blood in other villages, and he is glad there are none in his own village.

Political education in North Viet Nam, though repetitious, is not stagnant. After the defeat of the French and their withdrawal from Indo-China, the Americans became the capitalist-imperialist villains in Vinh's political-education sessions. Parallels were drawn between the French, who first came as traders and missionaries but later found pretexts for moving troops in and taking over Viet Nam, and the Americans, who sent "military advisers" to South Viet Nam in 1955 as a prelude to sending combat troops. "When the French pulled out, they gave way to the United States, which created a puppet government in the South," Vinh says. "The Americans, posing as advisers, pulled the strings of the government. They intended to get control of the South and use it as a springboard to attack the North. Eventually, finding that they couldn't take over the South that way, because of the heroic National Liberation Front, they came out in the open and brought in their troops. I have no doubt that their only motive is to take over the country. I can't imagine that the French and the Americans have different aims, because the Americans used to aid the French in Viet Nam. The Americans surely aren't pouring their men and resources in here for nothing. Russia and China, on the other hand, are helping the North simply because they are brotherly Socialist countries. They've sent us weapons and advisers but no troops. I think this shows that they don't want to take over our country. If we asked for troops, Russia, China, Cuba, Poland, and many other Socialist countries would be glad to send them, but we won't need them. If the Americans could control the South, they wouldn't be satisfied. They would attack the North. But we will succeed in liberating the South."

Although Vinh believes that the United States is a rich country, he has a low opinion of it. "From what I'm told," he says, "there are only a limited number of capitalists in the United States who are very rich, and the bulk of the population—the workers—lead a pretty miserable life compared to the capitalists. The workers, of course, aren't as badly off as workers elsewhere, because the living standard in the United States is higher than in most countries." Vinh's knowledge of the Soviet Union and China is also very limited. His political instructors told him that the Sino-Soviet ideological conflict began because Khrushchev started to deviate from the true Socialist ideology, and the Chinese were obliged to point that out to him. "Socialist doctrine should be a little flexible, to conform with local conditions, so Khrushchev may have been right, considering the special circumstances in his country," Vinh says. "We think it's better to stick to the principles of Socialism quite closely, however. For that reason, the North adheres to the Chinese more than to the Russians." Vinh does not know whether the Soviet Union or China gives North Viet Nam more aid, but he quotes a saying in the North that goes, "Anything China has we have, too." Vinh has heard that Khrushchev was ousted from power and is now a private citizen. He is familiar with the name of one of his successors—Kosygin, who visited North Viet Nam. He has heard nothing about Brezhnev, who stayed at home. He knows of Titov and Gagarin, the Russian cosmonauts; he has never been told that the Americans, too, have put men in space. Vinh knows the names of most of North Viet Nam's leaders; of two Americans, President Kennedy and President Johnson ("Johnson is the more ambitious and warlike"); of a number of Chinese leaders; and of General de Gaulle and several French generals who were involved in the First Indo-China War, including Brigadier General Christian Marie Ferdinand de la Croix de Castries, who commanded at Dien Bien Phu. "I don't know whether the French morally support us in this war or not, but I don't think they support the United States," Vinh says. "They had a bad experience here, so they must want to stay away from this mess." Vinh also knows the name of every South Vietnamese leader who has come to power since the assassination of President Ngo Dinh Diem.

There is no electricity in any of the homes in Vinh's hamlet. The only power line there operates two loudspeakers, over which Vinh and his neighbors received some of their political education. Radio Hanoi, the sole radio station in North Viet Nam, is piped over the loudspeakers for two to three hours at a time, usually four times a day, at just those times when the peasants aren't working in the fields: early in the morning, before work; at lunch-and-siesta time; and twice in the evening, before and after organizations hold

181

their meetings. Radio Hanoi presents news programs, special programs for workers, peasants, and young people, and music, but the music never includes love songs, which are the most popular kind of music in the South. "All our songs encourage production and the fighting spirit or celebrate the achievements of Socialist countries," Vinh says. Occasionally, the Radio Hanoi programs are interrupted by speeches or announcements from the hamlet authorities. The two loudspeakers are situated on the edge of the hamlet —one on a dike, the other in an open field. Although the nearest houses are some fifty yards away, everyone gets the full benefit of the broadcasts, for the loudspeakers are turned very high and can be heard beyond the borders of the hamlet. People who live near the loudspeakers are, in fact, something of a captive audience. "It's difficult for them to talk to each other in normal voices," Vinh says. "They get used to having to shout. The loudspeakers disturb people a little, but they're for the good of the majority. They're not a big issue. They don't make people very angry." There are five or six portable radios in Vinh's hamlet, which has a population of four hundred people. Only someone who has distinguished himself on community projects and who is judged politically reliable is allowed to buy a radio, and batteries are scarce and expensive. One of Vinh's friends had a radio, and he and Vinh and a few other people got together secretly and picked up forbidden stations late at night. They listened to Liberation Radio, the clandestine voice of the Viet Cong, and to Radio Saigon, the Voice of America, and the B.B.C.; they preferred the B.B.C. "It's all right in the countryside to listen to the programs you want to hear," Vinh says. "You can trust a few people." Once or twice a month, movies were shown in Vinh's hamlet. The technicians brought portable generators to run the projectors, and showed films that portrayed life in cooperatives, progress in other Communist countries, and scenes of the battle of Dien Bien Phu.

Vinh is a Buddhist by birth, but he has never gone to a pagoda to worship, and he took no part in religious activities at home. Though the population of his hamlet is entirely Buddhist, only the elderly residents go to the pagoda. Vinh has never been told not to believe in the Buddha or not to go to a pagoda. "Nobody makes an issue of religion," he says. "Religion isn't formally forbidden. It's just not fashionable to be devout." Vinh knows that a majority of Catholics in the North fled to the South during the three-hundred-day period of grace after the Geneva Agreements. He doesn't know precisely why they left; someone once told him that the Catholics believed their God had moved to the South. He senses that the Catholics who remained in the North still want to go to the South, but he doesn't know of any policy of discrimination against them. Vinh doesn't think that religion is disappearing in the North. "Buddhism is a pretty loose religion, so it doesn't matter much whether or not the young people go to the pagodas," he says. "Religion is really for elderly people. We'll go to the pagodas when we're older." Young people in the North are still studying to become priests and monks, and, as far as Vinh can judge, the régime doesn't plan to wipe out religion. He thinks that there will always be religions in the North, and that it would be a bad idea to have none. Vinh has never heard about anti-religious campaigns in other Communist countries, and he is not familiar with Karl Marx's famous dictum "Religion

183

is the opium of the people." "Only getting drunk, gambling, and divorce are considered bad," he says.

Teen-age marriages are also socially unacceptable in North Viet Nam; except with special permission, young men are not allowed to marry before they are twenty. Boys and girls are not permitted to be alone together in the dark under any circumstances. In the North, families no longer arrange marriages; young people choose their own marriage partners, and if they need any advice they receive it from one of the collective organizations. Vinh and the girl he married had known each other as children; they used to play with each other and fight with each other. A romance eventually flourished while they were working together in the youth organization. They were married in January, 1962, just three months before Vinh was drafted. Vinh didn't know at the time that he was about to go into the Army, but he would have got married even if he had known. "Marriage is something quite different from military service," he says. He and his bride lived with his brother in the brother's house until Vinh was drafted. Then his wife returned to her own home, and at present she is living with her widowed mother in the hamlet. She belongs to the cooperative organization, the youth organization, the women's organization, and the village militia, which now has more women than men in it, since so many of the men have been drafted. Vinh and his wife have no children. They hope someday to have three or four—no more than that. "The government has never told us to produce many children or few children," Vinh says. "It has simply advised us to space our children reasonably, so that each of them can be well taken care of. The government does not give us any medical advice. We are just told to exercise caution. If a couple produced seven children in seven years, they wouldn't be formally criticized. The wife would probably get some advice from the women's organization, and her husband might get some advice from one of the organizations he belonged to."

Vinh is proud of his country's achievements. For the last twelve years, the country has been run by Vietnamese, not by foreigners, and many factories have been built in his province in those years. When Vinh was a child, there were only a few primary schools, and they were expensive; there is now a free primary school in virtually every village. Critics of Communist régimes are not as impressed as Vinh is by the increased literacy in the North. They believe that the régime has educated the population merely as a way of indoctrinating it more thoroughly. A typical mathematics problem that students in a North Vietnamese school are asked to solve goes, "In a battle in which the gallant National Liberation Forces defeated the army of the American imperialists and their Vietnamese puppet troops, 840 enemy soldiers were killed. If ¼ of the dead were puppet troops and the rest of the dead were American imperialists, how many American imperialists were killed in the battle?" It will hardly occur to children brought up on lessons like this that they have political connotations, that the terms "American imperialists" and "puppet troops" are not objective, or that mathematics can be taught in terms of apples and oranges. The only thing that might surprise primary-school pupils in North Viet Nam would be a mathematics problem that dealt with a defeat suffered by the Viet Cong or the People's Army. They are never told of any such defeats.

Vinh thinks that most people in the North are happy

with the régime, even though the citizens of the Democratic Republic of Viet Nam are not free to do what they want. (Permission is required even for killing a pig.) "Collective work and a regimented life are matters of convenience," Vinh says. "People resent them at first, but after a time they realize the good they do for them. The government never forces the people to do anything without convincing them of its usefulness. That's why we have political education. There are many people who have a few personal complaints to make about things in the North, but only landlords and other formerly privileged people would prefer the kind of life they lived before 1954. President Ho has given us a new way of life, which is not perfect but is quite acceptable. We have been told—and I believe what I have been told—that people should not be given complete freedom to do as they please. Freedom results in social injustices and economic inequality. If we had more freedom, there would once again be rich, idle landlords and poor peasants who had nothing but their shabby huts. We have absolute political equality in the North now, and economically everyone is in about the same position as everyone else. We will soon achieve absolute economic equality, and I think that will be a very good thing."

In early March of 1962, there were thirty militiamen of draft age in Vinh's village, and they were all ordered to report to the nearby district town for a medical examination. On April 1st, Vinh learned that he and four other young men had been chosen to enter the Army immediately and were to serve two-year terms. The five draftees left their homes on April 10th and walked to the district town. There some officers of the 330th Independent Brigade, to which they had been assigned, met them and walked with them a few miles to one of the brigade's bases. The base was in a secluded area, and three battalions of men were stationed there, housed in large barracks. Arriving at the base late in the day, Vinh was given a good dinner and went to bed. The next morning, he was assigned to his battalion, company, platoon, and squad, and was issued two uniforms, two sets of underwear, two pairs of canvas boots, three pairs of socks, a helmet, a blanket, a mosquito net, a knapsack, a rice bowl, and a pair of chopsticks. Three days later, when the usual military paperwork was completed, Vinh's training began.

Six mornings a week, Vinh and the other recruits rose at five o'clock, did gymnastics, cleaned their quarters, washed, dressed, and ate breakfast. From six-thirty to eleven, they had military or political training. This was followed by lunch and a siesta, further military or political training from two to five-thirty, dinner at six, and "cultural activities" (reading, singing, or meetings) from seven to nine. Bedtime was at nine-thirty, and the half hour before it was free. Sundays were entirely free, and a third of the soldiers were allowed to go home for the day. Vinh went home only once during his first four months in the Army. "It was impractical to go home," he says. "Most of the day was lost on the road. Anyway, it's not good to go home, because it only makes you miss your family more and keeps you from doing your job well." Vinh received military training four days a week, political training twice a week. During his military training, he learned how to march, run, crawl, throw grenades, and handle Soviet and Chinese rifles. During his political training, he learned the responsibilities and duties of a soldier in the PAVN, or People's Army, and learned how Socialism

187

TEN / *Vietnamese*

functions, and more about the evils of capitalism and imperialism. Vinh did not prefer one form of training to the other, and was glad they alternated, because that way neither became monotonous.

Vinh followed this schedule at the base from April, 1962, until the beginning of August. Then he and eighty other recruits, who had shown leadership ability, were selected to attend a training course for noncommissioned officers. Being chosen was an honor that Vinh was reluctant to accept. "N.C.O.s have to stay in the Army a year longer than ordinary soldiers," he says. "I had hoped to go home after two years of military service. I didn't want to stay in for three years. I complained, but I was told I was needed." Vinh and the other N.C.O. candidates were sent a few miles by truck to a base in another district in Thanh Hoa. They learned to fire Soviet and Chinese submachine guns, to lead squads on scouting operations and in attacks, and to lay ambushes. In March, 1963, Vinh was promoted to corporal, and a month later he returned to his former station. Here he continued to receive political instruction from Army political commissars, but now he gave new recruits the same military training he had been given when he went into the Army. Vinh hadn't gone home at all during the N.C.O. course. He was able to go home twice between April, 1963, and January, 1964, but then the three battalions of the 330th Brigade were transferred about sixty-five miles north to a seaside camp in Thai Binh province, where they were taught how to defend the coast. Except for the last three months of 1964, when Vinh's unit was sent to repair irrigation dikes in the nearby province of Ninh Binh, he was at the seaside camp until March, 1965. During this period, he decided to try to join the Communist Party—a complicated process, which involved being observed and investigated by the Party. "Party members watch you for a period of at least a year to see if you fulfill your responsibilities competently and with a light heart," Vinh says. "If you complain about anything, even in your free time, that's held against you. One day, the squad I commanded was ordered to repair a certain section of broken dike. Another squad had to do the same amount of work on a different section of the dike. My squad did well and the other squad did pretty badly. In a criticism session held that night, I didn't bring the issue up, out of consideration for the other squad leader, so I was criticized for being sentimental and not having enough competitive spirit." At the time Vinh was captured, no action had been taken on his application to join the Party. He thinks he wasn't accepted into the Party partly because he hadn't yet met its high admission standards and partly because an uncle of his had fought with the French and had then become an abusive official; it is difficult for relatives of former reactionaries to get into the Party, Vinh says. He doesn't think he will make another attempt to join the Party, but he would be honored if he had a son who was admitted into the Party. "The Party makes policy, and if you belong to it you can really help your country," he says.

In August, 1964, Vinh was promoted to sergeant. Early in 1965, when he was looking forward to his discharge, his battalion was told that the National Liberation Front had appealed to North Viet Nam for assistance. Most of the soldiers, including Vinh, volunteered to go to the South. "I volunteered because I really wanted to help liberate the South, and also as a matter of self-respect," Vinh says. "I wanted to keep up with my contemporaries. Many soldiers were under social pressure from their friends to volunteer, and they also feared that they or their families would get into trouble if they didn't file applications asking to be sent to the South."

Vinh's application to go to the South was accepted, and in April, 1965, he left the 330th Brigade with sixty-five other volunteers. They first proceeded northwest, on foot, by train, and by truck, to join a fledgling battalion of the 325th Division. The battalion's base was in the jungle, in Hoa Binh province, and the young men received a two-month training course in jungle warfare there. In May, Vinh was granted a ten-day leave to see his wife—the first time he had been home since late 1963. Vinh didn't tell his wife of his imminent trip to the South. "I was afraid she would ask me to stay with her," he says. "I told her I was going on a distant assignment."

During his trip northwest in April, and on his way home in May, Vinh saw the ruins of many roads and bridges that had been destroyed by American planes; the United States had begun bombing North Viet Nam regularly on February 7th. "The officials in my village told the people to dig trenches," Vinh says. "They didn't have to teach the people how to dig them. They still remembered from the days of the French bombings. The people were angry about the bombings, because civilians were killed, and because the destruction of roads and bridges hampered traffic, interfering with their daily lives. I don't think they minded repairing the roads and bridges. The government asked them to do it for their own benefit. They were angry with those who did the bombing, not with the government. If the Americans eventually bomb Hanoi, it will make the people even angrier and more determined to fight." Vinh heard over Radio Hanoi of only two instances of civilians being killed or wounded by bombs, but he gathered from people he talked with and from the sight of wrecked homes near the demolished bridges that there had been many more. He thinks the radio did not report all the casualties, because such reports might have had a bad effect on morale. Before Vinh was captured, Radio Hanoi claimed that a thousand planes had been shot down over North Viet Nam—five times as many as the United States was aware it had lost at that time. One plane, hit by anti-aircraft fire, crashed into a marketplace a few miles from Vinh's village, killing seventy people. Some of the downed planes were put on exhibition at various places, and people walked miles to see them. Once, in the course of his travels, Vinh saw a captured American pilot being paraded through a hamlet. "He wasn't handcuffed," Vinh says. "He didn't look either cheerful or unhappy. He appeared indifferent. I didn't have a chance to talk with him, so I never found out what he was doing there. I just happened to see him."

On June 20th, Vinh's battalion, consisting of about four hundred men, set out for the South. Vinh's knapsack contained black pajamas, khaki uniforms, a hammock, a nylon sheet (to make a tent cover), some medicine, and some dried food. He also carried a canteen, a spade, a Chinese submachine gun, and a hundred rounds of ammunition. He wore sandals, because boots were unsuitable for the march south. While the battalion was still moving through the North, it marched at night, for security reasons, but mostly on main roads. On July 20, 1965, it crossed from Quang

Binh, North Viet Nam's southernmost province, into Laos.

The march south through Laos was arduous. Every day, Vinh's battalion walked from five in the morning until five in the afternoon, along trails, through dense jungle, and up and down mountains and steep hills; the jungle provided sufficient cover for daylight movement. Occasionally, the battalion crossed a road being built by North Vietnamese engineers through southern Laos to the South Vietnamese border. The soldiers rested for a few minutes every hour, and halted about one day a week. Many of them fell ill with malaria, and all of them sometimes went hungry. There were food stations set up from five to ten days march apart, but if the men lost time crossing a stream or some other obstacle they ran short of food. The battalion marched and slept spread out over a mile or two as a precautionary measure; the soldiers weren't bombed in Laos, but they saw the aftermath of a great deal of bombing—smashed huts, and patches of jungle burned or blasted bare by bombs and napalm. Every night, before climbing into their hammocks, slung between tree branches, they dug trenches for emergency shelter. The battalion had eleven political commissars along, but there was no political education during the march. "It's good to rest at night when you're tired," Vinh says.

At the end of August, the battalion crossed from Laos into the South Vietnamese province of Kontum, a mountainous, sparsely populated area in which the terrain was as difficult and travel as grueling as they had been in Laos. Once during the march through Kontum, which took three and a half weeks, an advance unit of the battalion was bombed; two men were killed and one was wounded. The battalion reached its destination, Binh Dinh province, in the last days of September. Most of Binh Dinh, a province that has mountains and jungles in the interior and a densely populated fertile delta along its coast, is controlled by the Viet Cong; the government holds only the provincial capital, Qui Nhon, and its vicinity, some government outposts, several district capitals, such as Bong Son, and a small number of villages. Vinh's battalion spent a month in Binh Dinh's patches of jungle, resting, receiving medical care, and getting accustomed to the terrain. Although the men moved a few miles every couple of days to conceal their whereabouts, life in Binh Dinh was much easier than it had been on the way south. Rice was bought locally, and the soldiers occasionally spent some time in the Viet Cong-held villages in their area.

At the end of October, the battalion moved to the province of Quang Ngai, which is immediately north of Binh Dinh and is similar to it geographically and militarily. The soldiers spent several weeks in the jungles of Quang Ngai, preparing for their first attack. The object of their attack was Thach Tru, one of three hamlets on the edge of the district capital of Mo Duc. According to their intelligence, Thach Tru was occupied by one company of South Vietnamese Ranger troops. One night in late November, three of the four companies in the battalion—Vinh's company was one of them—left their camps and set out separately for Thach Tru, where they planned to rendezvous and take the hamlet by surprise, overwhelming it with their superior forces. Several things went wrong. There were heavy rains that night, and the three companies lost touch with each other. Vinh's company reached Thach Tru slightly late; the two other companies were very late. Then, the South Vietnamese had somehow learned of the impending attack, and instead of finding just one Ranger company in Thach Tru the North Vietnamese found three; two companies of Rangers stationed in the two hamlets near Thach Tru had been brought in as reinforcements. The PAVN soldiers attacked at four o'clock in the morning—several hours later than had been planned. At seven, just as they fought their way through part of the defensive perimeter, daylight came, and with it fighter-bombers; the PAVN troops had to withdraw into the jungle. Twenty-one members of the battalion had been killed and about eighteen wounded. Vinh estimates that his platoon killed thirty Rangers; he doesn't know how many Rangers the other PAVN troops killed. Vinh himself, who was in charge of a squad, hit three South Vietnamese soldiers with his Chinese submachine gun. Once the men were back in the jungle, a battle critique was held, to enable the PAVN soldiers to learn from their mistakes. The officers and political commissars told them that the attack plan hadn't been kept secret (no one knew how the news of the attack had leaked out, though), and that the planning hadn't been sound, because the troops had arrived late. "We have to foresee everything, including rain," Vinh says.

Between battles, life in the insect-ridden jungles of Binh Dinh and Quang Ngai was not very agreeable, but to Vinh the morale seemed good. "I didn't suspect anyone in my unit of wishing to defect," he says. "There was only one man who was afraid of fighting. He pretended to be sick all the time. That man was criticized—that coward." The pay that Vinh and the other PAVN soldiers had received in the

North stopped when they volunteered to go south, and from April through November they were given no money. Then, starting in December, each of the soldiers received a few piasters a month—enough to buy some local tobacco, with which to roll their own cigarettes, or a few candies, or needles and thread for mending their clothes. They were warned against buying any American goods they found on sale, because these might be poisoned. Between battles, the soldiers on reserve had little diversion from the tedious routine of camp life. Occasionally, a few Viet Cong came and gave lectures on guerrilla fighting techniques. And occasionally, when there were no political commissars around, Vinh and his friends listened to the radio. "We weren't allowed to listen to the radio at all—not even Radio Hanoi or Liberation Radio," Vinh says. "The political commissars were afraid we would tune in to reactionary stations. They said you had to reach a certain stage of enlightenment so you could tell the difference between truth and falsehood. Apparently, we hadn't reached that stage yet. We sometimes listened to Radio Saigon anyway. It made a change, though the music they played didn't appeal to me. I've been educated to like instructive songs, so I didn't care for the love songs broadcast by Radio Saigon. We believed a few of Radio Saigon's news items, but not the reports that dealt with Thach Tru and other actions we'd taken part in, because they contradicted what we had seen with our own eyes. The radio tried to minimize the enemy's losses and exaggerate ours. Even Party members listened to the radio with us, and I wasn't afraid they'd betray us to the political commissars. We comrades-in-arms don't try to harm each other."

195

In early January of 1966, Vinh's battalion took part in its second action—again in Quang Ngai province. Several PAVN battalions mounted a night attack on the district capital of Minh Long and on two nearby outposts and three hamlets in which government troops were stationed. The PAVN troops fought their way into Minh Long and the hamlets without very much trouble, and held them for several days. They didn't try to occupy the two outposts; they just surrounded them and harassed the garrisons, in the hope of luring rescue troops into an ambush. Vinh's company prepared the ambush, but no government relief force ever arrived. The only help that the garrisons received came from some planes, which bombed the area for several days. One night, the members of the two garrisons tried to escape by slipping through the PAVN lines; they were all captured. After a few more days, when there seemed to be no hope of luring reinforcements into an ambush, Vinh's battalion withdrew. Ten men in the battalion had been killed during the Minh Long operation; Vinh doesn't know the exact number of South Vietnamese casualties, but the soldiers in the six government-held positions were all either killed or wounded or taken prisoner. The PAVN soldiers turned the prisoners over to the local Viet Cong guerrillas.

Vinh was not impressed by the South Vietnamese soldiers he fought against at Thach Tru and Minh Long. "Every soldier is afraid of death—even we Socialist troops are," he says. "But we are tougher than the enemy. If we have to defend a position, we'll fight to the last man; the troops in the two outposts just outside Minh Long tried to sneak away. At Thach Tru, we fought from an exposed position, yet we suffered fewer casualties than the enemy. We can always get the better of the enemy soldiers, except when they are supported by heavy artillery or effective airstrikes. Our chief aim in coming down here is to fight the Americans. We understand that Vietnamese puppet troops provide cover for American troops, and that we have to do away with the cover first. I'm not happy about killing Vietnamese soldiers, even though they don't fight very bravely. But then that is the Americans' scheme." (Despite Vinh's statement, neither the Viet Cong nor the North Vietnamese usually fight to the last man; they ordinarily retreat when they are attacked by a superior force. When it is possible, they will avoid fighting unless they believe the odds are heavily in their favor. And, having suffered heavy casualties in their initial clashes with the Americans, the Viet Cong and the North Vietnamese have shown a marked reluctance to challenge sizable United States units.)

Vinh was very favorably impressed by the Viet Cong. "I think the Liberation Forces are superior to the soldiers of the People's Army," he says. "They know the terrain better than we do, and they excel in hit-and-run attacks and in playing tricks on the enemy. We specialize in making frontal assaults, and have been trained to fight conventionally. We are not very good at guerrilla fighting. We may be able to catch up with them later, when we've had more experience fighting in the South."

Vinh's battalion stayed in the jungles of Quang Ngai for about two weeks after the Minh Long engagement, and then moved back into Binh Dinh. They reached one of their base areas in mid-January, shortly before Tet, the lunar New Year, which is the major Vietnamese holiday. They spent most of Tet, a week-long festival, in Viet Cong-held villages in northern Binh Dinh. Each of the PAVN soldiers was given a few piasters, and they pooled their resources to buy some pigs for a feast. Both sides had declared a three-and-a-half-day ceasefire from the eve of Tet to the third day after Tet. "Each side agreed to shoot only if it was attacked," Vinh says. "We didn't expect to be attacked. The local population told us the puppet troops had observed the Tet truce scrupulously in previous years, because they liked to celebrate Tet peacefully by getting drunk and gambling. Our political commissars told us that the Americans would honor the truce, too. They said that we shouldn't attack any Vietnamese troops but that we should attack the American imperialists if there was a good opportunity, because Tet is a Vietnamese festival, not an American one."

Vinh's unit did not attack the Americans during Tet. A week after Tet ended, American and South Vietnamese soldiers launched a large-scale offensive in northern Binh Dinh. The brunt of the attack fell on the villages in Hoai Nhon district, where Vinh's unit was staying. On January 28, his company was ordered to take up a position along Main Highway 1, north of Bong Son, the district capital, and to harass the attackers in an attempt to lure them into an ambush set by another PAVN company. Vinh was leading a platoon of nineteen men. As soon as his platoon was astride the main road, fighter-bombers appeared and pinned it down. The airstrikes lasted for several hours. The position seemed untenable, and Vinh was ordered to withdraw his platoon and join another unit. Some of Vinh's men had been scattered by the bombing, so he told his deputy to lead the bulk of the platoon away while he stayed behind to round up the stragglers. As Vinh was carrying his submachine gun and two weapons abandoned by wounded soldiers, he was surrounded by South Vietnamese troops. He realized that he was trapped, and hid two of the weapons in some brush. As he was considering shooting his way out and wondering whether his muddy submachine gun would function, he was shot in both arms and fell to the ground. The South Vietnamese soldiers then seized him.

Vinh was handcuffed, given first aid, blindfolded, and taken by Jeep to the police station in Bong Son, where he was interrogated for five days. During the first twenty-four hours of the interrogation period, he was questioned unremittingly. Then he was allowed a few hours sleep before the interrogation resumed. Most of the questions he was asked dealt with purely military subjects. Although Vinh knew that discussing military matters was against PAVN regulations, he decided to give his interrogators all the information he had about his unit. "I decided to talk, because my battalion was always on the move, so I didn't think it really mattered if I disclosed its former whereabouts, and also because I was badly beaten," Vinh says. He was hit on the chest with wooden clubs and rubber truncheons, slapped in the face, and pummeled on the head and back, but he wasn't beaten quite as badly as some of the other prisoners were. He thinks one reason he got off more lightly was that he was wounded, and another reason was that he was in a state of shock from having been bombed for several hours. He suspects that because he was temporarily dazed his interrogators considered him a little bit demented. No Americans questioned him at Bong Son.

After five days in Bong Son, Vinh was flown to Qui Nhon, the capital of Binh Dinh province (it was his first plane ride), along with a soldier from his company who had been captured a few hours later. Vinh spent more than three weeks in the Qui Nhon jail, with a mixed bag of prisoners— captured Viet Cong, hoodlums, and curfew violators. He was not interrogated at Qui Nhon. He thinks he was held there until transportation to Saigon became available, for he was presently flown to Saigon, where he has been held since the beginning of March.

Vinh shares a tiny, hot room at a Vietnamese Army interrogation center with three other PAVN prisoners. The room has only one bed, and no reed sleeping mats or mosquito nets. The prisoner who feels weakest on any given night sleeps on the bed. The others sleep on the concrete floor. The prisoners are given two meals a day—lunch and dinner—and one shower a week. Vinh has only his three roommates for company except at mealtimes, when the forty North Vietnamese prisoners who are being kept at the center eat together and are allowed to chat. Vinh has been interrogated frequently since his arrival in Saigon, usually by Vietnamese Army intelligence officers but occasionally by Americans. When he is interrogated by Vietnamese officers, he is often beaten or tortured with electrodes. Some of his comrades have been more severely beaten and tortured with electrodes, and several of them have fainted during the interrogation sessions. Vinh thinks he is still receiving milder treatment than his comrades because of his wounds (the bandages have just come off, and both arms are badly scarred) and because his Bong Son interrogators wrote on his record that he was dense and his statements were therefore not to be taken very seriously. American officers who have questioned him have sometimes threatened to beat him, but they haven't done so. The Vietnamese have often beaten him prior to his interrogation by Americans. When a Vietnamese has started to beat Vinh in the presence of Americans, the Americans have quietly left the room— except on two occasions, when they stayed. Some of Vinh's fellow-prisoners have concluded that the Americans consider themselves too dignified to beat people, and let their "lackeys" do it for them, but Vinh thinks that the Americans have simply behaved well, as "respectable foreigners." He is inclined to believe what he has always been told in the North—that individual Americans are decent and only the American government's policy is bad.

Vinh has been approached several times by Vietnamese psychological-warfare officers. On one occasion, they asked him to write a letter to his wife, which would be read in radio broadcasts beamed to the North. Vinh agreed to do so, and began his letter with a greeting that is customary in North Viet Nam: "May Socialism be established and strengthened in our dear country." He was beaten for writing that, and was instructed to start a new letter, omitting the greeting. He refused. "I wasn't praising Socialism," he says. "I was just wishing it would thrive." The letter-writing project went no further. On another occasion, Vinh was asked to say some nice things about life in the South and discredit some aspects of life in the North in a tape-recorded interview, which was to be broadcast to the North. Again Vinh agreed. The psychological-warfare officers wanted him to state that he was disillusioned with Communism, and that the hardships the North Vietnamese soldiers had to endure in the South were intolerable, so that their morale was very low. "In the interview, I never tried to embellish life in the

North or to attack things in the South, but I didn't want to embellish the situation in the South, either," Vinh says. "Apparently, I didn't say what they wanted me to, for I was beaten up several times. I can only say what I really think and believe."

Vinh thinks his interrogation is almost completed. He has been told alternately that he will be sent to a permanent prison camp outside Saigon, that he will be killed, and that he will be allowed to go home. No one has asked him to become a defector, and he has no intention of defecting. If he had his choice of things to do while he was in prison, he would like to learn English. "It's a universal language," he says. "It's not exclusively the language of the American imperialists. Chinese and Russian are not so widely spoken." He is given nothing to do, however, and nothing to read. If he could obtain some newspapers, he would prefer North Vietnamese to South Vietnamese papers. Vinh knows that prisoners in the North are asked to give radio interviews, and he has seen the American pilot on parade; therefore he accepts the treatment he is accorded, though he resents the beatings and the torture.

Vinh misses his wife. By now, he thinks, she has probably learned he is in the South, but she may not know that he is a prisoner. The other soldier from Vinh's company who was taken prisoner near Bong Son told Vinh that the unit had been looking for him and that he has probably been listed as missing in action. Vinh would rather go home than stay in the South, even if his wife should be brought down and he should be given plenty of money. "There is too much inequality here, too many injustices," he says.

"As I was taken through Saigon, I saw so many shabby people walking on the streets and so many well-dressed people driving around in big shiny cars. There are so many beggars, and I've seen orphans on the streets. In the North, we have no beggars, and orphans are properly taken care of. In the villages in the South, some people don't have enough to eat and others have too much. I feel that I would be out of place here. I'm used to life in the North. It's better for all to be poor and equal than for some to be rich and live comfortably while others are miserable." Vinh admits that people in the South have a generally higher standard of living than people in the North, but he is confident that the standard of living in the North will improve. He assumes that if he is eventually allowed to go home he will be thrown in jail and kept there for some time, but he believes that in the end the authorities will realize that he is loyal and will release him. "If there is no war by then, I'll return to civilian life," he says. "No one enjoys a military career. If there's still a war and if I still have the confidence of my superiors, I'll volunteer to come south again. I believe that if we don't succeed in liberating the South, the Americans will get the upper hand. Imperialists are never satisfied, and if they could get their hands on the South, they would invade the North."

Although there were over two hundred thousand American troops in South Viet Nam at the time of his capture, Vinh believes that the North will win the war. "I didn't change my mind when I was in the jungle or when I saw so many airplanes and was confronted by so much firepower on the enemy side," he says. "In spite of the enemy's weapons and technological advantages, I think we will win the war, because there is more to this war than bombs and artillery. Might alone doesn't count. Our war is a people's war and a war for a just cause."

A NOTE ABOUT THE AUTHOR: *Susan Sheehan* is a writer on the staff of *The New Yorker*. Her articles have appeared not only in *The New Yorker* but also in *The New Republic*, *Harper's Magazine*, and other publications. She is married to Neil Sheehan, a reporter for *The New York Times*, and lives in Washington, D. C.

A NOTE ON THE TYPE: The text of this book is set in Electra, a typeface designed by W(illiam) A(ddison) Dwiggins for the Mergenthaler Linotype Company and first made available in 1935. Electra cannot be classified as either "modern" or "old style." It is not based on any historical model, and hence does not echo any particular period or style of type design. It avoids the extreme contrast between "thick" and "thin" elements that marks most modern faces, and is without eccentricities which catch the eye and interfere with reading. In general, Electra is a simple, readable typeface which attempts to give a feeling of fluidity, power, and speed.

W. A. Dwiggins (1880–1956) was born in Martinsville, Ohio, and studied art in Chicago. In 1904 he moved to Hingham, Massachusetts, where he built a solid reputation as a designer of advertisements and as a calligrapher. He began an association with the Mergenthaler Linotype Company in 1929, and over the next twenty-seven years designed a number of book types of which Metro, Electra, and Caledonia have been used very widely. In 1930 Dwiggins became interested in marionettes, and through the years made many important contributions to the art of puppetry and the design of marionettes.

The book was composed by Brown Bros. Linotypers, Inc., New York, N. Y., printed and bound by The Book Press, Inc., Brattleboro, Vt.